THE WAVE THREE WAY TO BUILDING YOUR DOWNLINE

Richard Poe

PRIMA PUBLISHING

All income claims made in this book by individual distributors are true, to the author's best knowledge. In no case did these distributors represent or imply to the author that their incomes were typical for the industry, or for their companies, nor does the author so claim. On the contrary, the author selected interview subjects specifically for their outstanding and unusual achievements.

All companies mentioned or profiled in this book were selected by the author solely for the purpose of illustration. All are successful and reputable companies, to the author's best knowledge, but in no case should the inclusion of any company in this book be interpreted as an endorsement or recommendation by the author.

The publisher and the author explicitly do not endorse or recommend any particular network marketing company, and urge those readers who are searching for an MLM opportunity to conduct their own thorough due diligence before risking their time or their money. Given the inherently risky nature of business, the publisher and author further disclaim any warranty, expressed or implied, regarding the financial results from use of the methods, advice, systems, or information contained in this book.

© 1997 by Richard Poe

Library of Congress Cataloging-in-Publication Data

Poe, Richard.
    The wave three way to building your downline / Richard Poe.
        p.   cm.
    Includes index.
    ISBN 0-7615-0439-7
    1. Multilevel marekting.   I. Title.
HF5415.126.P635   1996
658.8'4—dc20   96-32432
                                                                                   CIP

97 98 99 00 01 HH 10 9 8
Printed in the United States of America

How to Order

Single copies may be ordered from Prima Publishing, P.O. Box 1260BK, Rocklin, CA 95677; telephone (916) 632-4400. Quantity discounts are also available. On your letterhead, include information concerning the intended use of the books and the number of books you wish to purchase. Visit us online at http://www.primapublishing.com

To my wife, Marie,
my friend, my Muse,
and my true love

CONTENTS

FOREWORD

If it hadn't been for Richard Poe, thousands—perhaps millions—of people would never have heard of network marketing. Including me. Richard used to have the office next to mine at *Success* magazine. As I recall, at least twice a week, as I was scurrying around taking care of some urgent triviality connected with a story I was writing, he would snag me in the hallway and lure me within to deliver an enthusiastic lecture on some new business trend he had just discovered that, he was sure, was destined to change history. It always started the same way.

"Duncan!" he would call slyly from his office door. "Would you like to take a look at something?"

It sounded innocuous. But behind his earnest spectacles, Richard couldn't quite conceal a grin. It was a trap, and we both knew it. If I gave in to my curiosity and went into his office, my afternoon was almost certainly shot. But I gave in often, because Richard was often right.

On one otherwise uneventful afternoon in 1990, after once again suckering me into his office, Richard pointed to a couple of large-format paperback books on a shelf.

"Do you know what those are?" he asked gravely.

I didn't.

"Take a look and tell me what you see," he instructed.

They were photo albums of some sort. On each page was a soft-focus picture of a couple—obviously married, and posing in formal dress—with a story of how they'd struggled from poverty or difficulty to remarkable wealth through something referred to as "the plan." They were homey, wholesome, Middle-American couples—white, black; short, tall; thin, plump; old, young. They all seemed very happy. All were associated, in some way, with a company called Amway, whose name had a vaguely familiar ring, but which I really knew nothing about.

"You don't read about people like this in business magazines," Richard's lecture began. On the contrary, he averred, editors at business magazines write mostly about the kind of people they know. They write about people with trust funds and Harvard MBAs; corporate presidents with multimillion-dollar golden parachutes; people who take taxicabs to work and feverishly watch the Dow Jones average along with their fat intake; celebrities who dabble in business by putting their likenesses on salad dressing bottles; and 60s radicals who run smallish companies that manufacture undistinguished but "ecologically friendly" products. In short, business magazines seem to feature everyone *except* network marketers. Their coverage spans every continent of the world, except the continent called Middle America.

"What if I told you that most business editors are writing about the wrong people?" said Richard. "What if I told you that the future belongs to people like those in this book? To the real Americans? That people like these are destined to be the backbone of the twenty-first-century economy?"

The bait taken, Richard calmly sprang the trap. He ripped some manuscript pages from his dot-matrix printer. It was the latest edition of his back-page column, "The Pulse," an article about people just like the ones in the book. Which he wanted me to edit. Now.

Today, virtually everyone involved in network marketing has a copy of that column—likely as not, a fifth-generation photocopy—which was entitled "Network Marketing: The Most Powerful Way to Reach Consumers in the '90s." As soon as the issue reached subscribers, our office telephones and fax machine went berserk for three weeks. In his column, Richard took the idea of network marketing seriously and described its power and potential. It was the first time a journalist had done that for decades—or perhaps ever—and network marketing people responded. Some of our fellow editors at *Success* were less than thrilled. Most editors I have met here in New York City look down on selling. To them, selling is an embarrassing, blue-collar vice, and Richard's network marketing coverage seemed an invasion of crass capitalism into that comfortable bastion of cleverness and art that we call an editorial office. To some of our colleagues, (none of whom work at *Success* anymore, by the way), MLM, franchising, infomercials and real estate—or really, anything that involved selling—seemed like the sort of get-rich-quick scams that Ralph Cramden might have gotten himself into on an episode of *The Honeymooners.*

Network marketing is anathema to many people who work in the established media because it seems loud and messy. It involves people looking after themselves, rejecting the benign rule of corporate and government bureaucrats. As they see it, independent business favors aggressive people who exploit others and talk too much about God, family, and country, and probably listen to country-western music.

In short, it took real guts for Richard to insist, as he did, through meeting after ice-cold meeting, that the magazine ought to go forward with a major MLM cover story.

Editor-in-Chief and Publisher Scott DeGarmo was understandably cautious. He listened skeptically to both sides, and decided to wait—to see if our readers kept up their interest in network marketing. After a year of lobbying from Richard and me, and scores of letters from *Success* readers demanding more network marketing coverage, Scott leapt in with both feet. He assigned Richard and me to put together what would soon become the first positive cover story on network marketing ever published by a national business magazine. "We Create Millionaires" ran in March 1992 and immediately sold twice as many copies on the newsstand as any issue we had ever printed. All of this fuss and furor now seems like ancient history. Today, every single issue of *Success* addresses network marketing, and we always mention an MLM article on our cover. Network marketing people are a constituency of the magazine. Unfortunately, the man who got all of this rolling in the first place has long since left *Success*. Richard Poe discovered he could write bestselling books such as *Wave Three* and *The Einstein Factor*, and finds being a successful author habit-forming. Hence you hold *The Wave Three Way* in your hands. And hence it has fallen to me to plan and edit *Success* magazine's network marketing material each month.

My life is very different now. Covering this industry over the last four years, I have felt, at times, as if I were living back in the year 1849, and that I'm the only journalist in the country writing about this amazing Gold Rush taking place in California. Most business editors get excited when they find a company whose sales or profits have "soared" 20 percent in the last year. I don't even look at a network marketing firm for a story unless its sales are growing by at least 100 percent annually. And even among those, I have to pick and choose. If you're supposed to be writing nonfiction, as I am, it's all a bit surreal.

While the mainstream media slept, network marketing penetrated mainstream American life and business. The largest insurance company in the U.S., Travelers, with $1.3 billion in annual revenues, sells its policies and investments entirely by network marketing. Excel Telecommunications, on track to hit $1 billion in sales this year, just went public at $27 per share; its stock hit $47 the same day. Many conventional corporations have MLM divisions or operations—although they typically are quiet about them. MCI sells long distance service through Amway. Colgate Palmolive has an MLM division called Jafra Cosmetics. TIME Inc. sells books through TIME-LIFE Direct. Only in this past year has the mainstream media finally begun to catch on—prodded, I suspect, by *Success*. In its November 6 1995 issue, *Forbes* magazine rated Nature's Sunshine, a public nutritional supplements company that did $300 million in 1995 sales, as one of the best small companies in America. In its very positive profile, *Forbes* even went so far as to describe Nature's Sunshine's MLM marketing plan without once resorting to the word "scam."

The Wall Street Journal has published a number of articles on MLM telephone resellers, MLM satellite TV networks and the growing "white-collar flight" to network marketing careers. *Household and Personal Products Industry* (HAPPI) magazine ranked Amway—with $7.2 billion in annual retail sales—among the top 5 companies by sales in the personal products industry, blowing past a number of household names, such as Estée Lauder, Revlon, Dial, and Bristol-Myers Squibb.

Even *The New York Times* published an article on former white-collar executives entering network marketing and matching their earlier incomes. Dated January 28, 1996, the headline read: "Many Exchange a Briefcase for the Sample Case of Sales." I must say the theme of that article bore an uncanny resemblance to a cover story I wrote with Executive Editor Michael Warshaw for *Success*'s December 1995 issue, which appeared about two months before the *Times* piece. That December issue, in which we re-used the cover line "We Create Millionaires," sold more at the newsstand than any previous issue in *Success*'s century of existence. I hope the January 28 *Times* did as well.

Why are mainstream journalists finally beginning to stir from their naps to discover network marketing—five years after *Success* magazine made the wake-up call? The answer, I think, is that the industry has just become too successful to ignore any longer. Several trends are making MLM companies more powerful, easier to operate, and more appealing to people with education and business sophistication. For this reason, I think general interest in the industry is about to skyrocket. These trends include:

- A growing population of refugees from America's largest corporations who are looking for a potentially lucrative business of their own.

- The increased competition and squeezing of profit margins in all the professions: doctors, dentists, lawyers, architects, CPAs.

- The proliferation of communications and database technologies: Telephones, computers and fax machines have replaced the car trunk as a selling tool.

- The increasing number of consumers content to buy through mail-order or by dialing a telephone.

- The growth of home-based businesses, as the home computer replaces the ledger book.

- The new baby boom, and the growing determination of white-collar Americans to reclaim their family lives.

The new converts to MLM include some of the most credible members of society. In the past year, Mike Warshaw has begun helping me research network marketing. We have interviewed numerous executives and corporate lawyers who have replaced or bettered their earlier incomes by working at home in network marketing. They brag that they no longer own business suits. We have met doctors and dentists who have gone into MLM to counter the income squeeze they are suffering at the hands of HMOs. We know successful entrepreneurs and even elected officials who have jumped in because they couldn't argue with the economics of network marketing. Some of these white-collar network marketers have formed their own companies to distribute products and services—from health supplements to discounted long-distance phone service. Most have simply joined existing firms to build their own selling organizations.

These are winners who have resources and skills. They can choose any career. They are sophisticated minds from the "real world" of business who analyzed the network marketing phenomenon and recognized an opportunity too good to pass up. Their imprimatur gives a new credibility to the industry.

Sometimes I wonder how long it will be before my former colleagues at *Success*—who argued so vehemently against MLM coverage five years ago—will pull up to my house in stretch limos to tell me about some great new opportunity they've gotten involved with.

The trends fueling the explosive growth of network marketing over the past 15 years are still accelerating. One of the most promising is MLM's overseas growth. International MLM organizations are easier to grow, the big distributors tell me, because Europeans and Asians are more open and less jaded to opportunity than Americans. Most of the world has had its commerce so tightly regulated, people are glad for a change, and many of them have disposable income for the first time in history. In addition, there's no mass retail distribution in Asia, South America or Eastern Europe: no Wal Mart, no Sears, just mom and pop stores and some isolated department stores with limited choices and high prices. Network marketing will become the mass retailer in much of the world—as it already has in Japan, where there are more than $20 billion in annual MLM sales.

Network marketing companies in services will continue to grow—long-distance service, travel, legal services, Internet hookups, electric power, you name it. The next decade could see the biggest portion of the U.S. marketplace move from the storefront to the telephone, through network marketing.

Perhaps the most important trend fueling the growth of MLM is one we might call The Family Fights Back. Unwilling to settle for the starved, frenetic home life of two-income households, and determined to remake modern family life more to their liking, a great many network marketing families are consciously re-creating the pioneer model, where life—including work—is based at home. Instead of flintlocks and subsistence agriculture, their tools are those of today's business frontier: the telephone, the computer, the modem, and the arts of public speaking and sales management. This point was brilliantly made in Nicole Biggart's academic study of direct selling culture, entitled *Charismatic Capitalism*. The freedom of network marketing in today's America is the freedom of the frontier 150 years ago: to stretch yourself beyond what you thought were your limits, to take your own chances, to join with family and friends to build something of your own.

So, who else was introduced to network marketing by Richard Poe, besides me? One young man at Yale Law School first discovered it in Richard's 1990 column and decided to join one of the companies mentioned. The income helped him work his way through law school. A few years later, that same young man, Mr. Ray Faltinsky, started his own MLM company called FreeLife in Milford, Connecticut. FreeLife did $12 million in wholesale sales its first year, has 30,000 distributors and is on track for $25 million this year.

At every single network marketing event I attend for *Success*—conventions, seminars and meetings with the industry's biggest players—a company founder or major distributor invariably confides in me that if I want to understand this industry, I must read the best book written on it, called *Wave Three* by Richard Poe. Two weeks ago, I talked to the young CEO of a network marketing company with $100 million in annual wholesale sales who told me he had based his growth strategy on the principles in *Wave Three.*

Just last week, I got a call from a distributor, a middle-aged woman, who mentioned in passing that *Wave Three* had changed her life. I asked why. She said, "It showed me the trends that were making network marketing grow so fast. I realized the company I was with wasn't on the ball. I was able to find another one that was, and was treating its people better."

As I write this, two years after its publication, *Wave Three* has just debuted on *Business Week* magazine's bestseller list—a remarkable achievement for a book that was sold not through splashy ads, expensive author tours, or reviews in prestigious journals, but by word of mouth. To my knowledge, *Wave Three* is the first general-interest book on network marketing ever to achieve official bestseller status (excepting, of course, the handful of autobiographies and self-help manifestoes by various MLM company founders, which are bought mainly by their tens of thousands—in some cases, millions—of loyal distributors).

It is my privilege to introduce you to my dear friend and comrade-in-arms—who wasn't afraid to tell a mistrustful world that there was real gold in the hills of network marketing, and to help bring our business experts into the Information Age.

To find an original business thinker who is also a skilled storyteller is almost unknown—but I don't know anyone who, having started to read one of Richard Poe's books, has ever been able to put it down before finishing it. In addition to being a practical book on how to build a business, *The Wave Three Way to Building Your Downline* is a riveting story of personal heroism, powerful ideas, and the triumph of the human spirit, told through the lives of the everyday pioneers of network marketing.

Duncan Maxwell Anderson
Senior Editor, *Success* magazine

ACKNOWLEDGMENTS

In the writing of this book I am indebted, above all, to my wife, Marie, for her inspiration, encouragement, and endless patience.

I thank all the crew at Prima Publishing, especially Jennifer Basye Sander and Ben Dominitz, whose idea this book really was, and my project editor, Betsy Towner, for her diligence, patience, and flexibility. Special gratitude goes to my friends at *Success* magazine, Duncan Maxwell Anderson and Scott DeGarmo, who have done so much to publicize my books, and to my many network marketing advisors, among whom John Milton Fogg, Len Clements (800-688-4766), Corey Augenstein, publisher of *MLM Insider* magazine (305-538-9077), and Michael S. Clouse have been especially helpful.

I also thank my brother Randy—a bona fide mathematical genius—who revealed to me the formula used in Chapter 1 for calculating the number of relationships in an MLM downline.

Finally, I thank all the wonderful people in the MLM industry, both those mentioned in this book and those who were left out, who gave generously of their time, their wisdom, and their experience, and without whose input *The Wave Three Way to Building Your Downline* would never have come into being.

INTRODUCTION

One night back in 1990, I stayed late in my office at *Success* magazine in order to listen to an audiotape adaptation of the book *Think and Grow Rich* by Napoleon Hill. At that time, I had not yet read any of Hill's books and had only the vaguest idea of who he was. Of course, I knew that Hill was considered one of the great motivators of all time, alongside such giants as Norman Vincent Peale, Dale Carnegie, and W. Clement Stone. I knew that he had been the editor of *Success* in past years. I even knew that he was credited with the famous aphorism, "If you can conceive it and believe it, you can achieve it."

But until I listened to that tape set, sitting alone well past midnight in a dark and deserted magazine office on New York City's Madison Avenue, I had never fully grasped the power and majesty of Hill's teachings, nor had I understood what a privilege it was to serve as senior editor at a magazine that, more than any other, represented Hill's legacy.

The following morning, when Editor-in-Chief and Publisher Scott DeGarmo arrived bright and early from his morning workout, I greeted him from my office, still wobbly from sleeplessness and reeling from the impact of Hill's astonishing ideas.

"I just spent most of the night listening to *Think and Grow Rich*," I confessed to Scott in a half whisper. "It's the most amazing thing I've ever heard!"

Scott broke into a wide grin and thrust out his hand. "Congratulations!" he declared. "Now you're finally beginning to understand what we're all about here. I wish some of my other editors would follow your example!"

Ever since that night, I have come to realize that humanity is sharply divided between those who have read and loved Napoleon Hill and those who have not. I have come, moreover, to appreciate the lonely battle that Scott DeGarmo, Duncan Anderson, and a handful of other dedicated souls at *Success* fight every day to keep that legacy burning bright in a cynical magazine marketplace concerned more with celebrity covers and glamorous liquor ads than with the core values that made America great.

It is surely no accident that *Success* magazine has become the first (and, so far, the only) national business journal to present regular coverage of the network marketing industry. Like Napoleon Hill, network marketing is concerned with a different America from the one you see when you walk down Madison Avenue. It's an America where faith, honor, and decency still abound, where pluck and persistence bring incredible rewards, where hard work pays off in the end and dreams still come true.

Like myself and my former colleagues from *Success* (I left the magazine in 1992 to become a full-time author), Hill started out as a journalist. He was fortunate to live during a time when giants walked the earth—men like Andrew Carnegie, Henry Ford, F. W. Woolworth, John D. Rockefeller—and ended up interviewing many of them for his books.

In this present volume, I have striven to imitate Hill's methodology to the best of my ability. By interviewing the top achievers of his day, Hill discovered and described the key principles which led to their success. Similarly, I have rooted out many of the core principles of network marketing success through extended interviews with many of that industry's most successful and articulate practitioners. Of course, I am no Hill and this book is no *Think and Grow Rich.* But if I have succeeded, even slightly, in reminding modern readers that Hill's spirit lives on through the men and women of network marketing, then I have surely done enough.

Through my study of network marketing leaders, I have uncovered a number of powerful principles and techniques, which I have collectively named the Wave Three Way and have described in these pages. Among them are the following seven principles and techniques:

- The Butterfly Effect: That mysterious characteristic of MLM downlines that enables network marketers to achieve massive results through minimal personal effort.

- Low-Pressure Prospecting: How to win recruits without even trying.

- Duplicatability: How to turbocharge your growth by keeping things simple.

- Catching Big Fish: How to build a huge downline by recruiting heavy hitters who will build it *for* you.

- Auto-Prospecting: Using video mailings and Internet Web sites to prospect while you sleep.

- Setting goals: How to set goals that will excite *you*, not just your sponsor.

- Training by Example: Exploiting auto-training systems that do 75 percent of your training for you.

Above all, this is a book about heroes and heroines— ordinary people who have achieved the extraordinary. In the six years that I have spent interviewing and profiling the men and women of network marketing, my admiration for this hardy breed has only continued to grow. Among them, I have found courage to match that of any war hero, intellect more piercing than that of many Fortune 100

CEOs, and hearts that are recklessly brimming with compassion, enthusiasm, and generosity. They are, in short, some of the finest people I know, worthy heirs to the Fords, the Carnegies, and the Woolworths whose stories so inspired Napoleon Hill. My only hope is that the words on these pages may do some small measure of justice to their incredible saga.

Chapter 1

THE BUTTERFLY EFFECT

I'm sorry to have to tell you this, Sue," said the man, "but we've given your sales territory to Samantha. You've been laid off."

Sue Grigsby was suddenly glad she hadn't ordered any breakfast that morning. Her stomach hung in her belly like a three-ton stone. As she stared at her regional manager across the table, all she could think was, "Be professional. Don't break down in front of him." But that was easier said than done. Sue could feel the blood burning in her face. Never in her life had she felt so ashamed.

Only a few months before, Sue Grigsby had single-handedly brought in one-fourth of the company's sales in the entire state of Connecticut. But that was all forgotten now. The recession had hit Sue's company hard. Once the second-largest gift wholesaler in the world, the firm was now struggling for bare survival. Sales were plummeting in every territory, including Sue's. The head office had responded in the only way it knew—with layoffs. Lots of them. Paranoia had spread through the sales force for months. Hardly a week went by without some colleague of Sue's getting the ax. Even so, Sue had thought she was immune. Never did she imagine it would actually happen to her.

"As I drove home from that meeting," Sue recalls, "I was numb, absolutely numb. My chest felt paralyzed. My arms felt paralyzed. More than anything else, I felt humiliated. It was as if I'd been rejected as a human being."

A Secret Advantage

As she drove home that morning, frozen with shame and fear, Sue Grigsby seemed doomed to take her place as one more tragic statistic of the 1990s—over 50, out of work, and divorced. Would she grow old and sick, Sue wondered, flitting from one temp job to the next? Would the year 2000 find her broke and desperate, elbowed out of the workforce by the young, the aggressive, and the computer savvy?

On that cold October morning, Sue Grigsby's worst fears seemed on the brink of realization. Her despair was echoed by tens of millions of other downsized workers across America. But, unlike so many others, Sue Grigsby possessed a secret advantage.

Sue herself did not yet realize it. She never suspected the awesome power that lay, even then, hovering at her fingertips, awaiting her command. But there it lay in abundance, power sufficient to free Sue forever from the chains of nine-to-five employment, power that could banish fear, transform her life, and bring every dream to fruition. Sue had only to activate that mighty force and let it work. It was called the Butterfly Effect.

MASSIVE RESULTS THROUGH MINIMAL ACTION

Scientists have theorized that a single butterfly flapping its wings on one side of the earth could create a chain reaction of turbulence through the atmosphere that could grow to a raging hurricane on the other side of the earth.

They call this the Butterfly Effect. It's just another way of saying that in complex systems like the weather, *massive results* can be achieved through *minimal actions*. It is the Butterfly Effect that makes weather so unpredictable. Despite all their satellites and high-tech equipment, meteorologists still cannot say for sure whether it will rain next weekend.

That's because the atmosphere is *complex*. It contains so many discrete particles of dust, water, and gas and so many currents, countercurrents, and microcurrents, all interacting with each other independently across the planet, that no scientist can hope to account for the actions of each hidden variable in the system.

But the only way to predict the weather is to first account for all those variables! You simply can't foretell the big events—such as hurricanes, heat waves, and thunderstorms—unless you first keep track of all the trillions of tiny microevents. The tiniest change in the sequence could alter the whole outcome.

Unlimited Power

Consider what would happen if we could somehow invent a computer powerful enough to calculate simultaneously every interaction between every particle in the Earth's atmosphere. We would then find ourselves in control of an immense power.

We could use this computer to predict the effects that even the tiniest action might eventually have on global weather, years in advance. By knowing the future in such detail, we would then gain the power to *alter* that future. Simply by standing in the right place and at the right time, we could, with a few deft waves of a feather, deliberately kick off a chain of events that could alter the weather exactly to our desire. We could, for example, set off a chain reaction that would eventually dump 18 inches of perfectly powdered snow on our favorite ski slope. Or we could turn a deadly hurricane in its path, sending it harmlessly out to sea.

The key would be knowing precisely the right place and the right time to wave that feather.

Gut Instinct

Of course, we may never have a computer capable of such detailed calculation. And altering the weather may be an overly ambitious goal. But, in more modest areas, people have been applying the Butterfly Effect, for centuries, with remarkable success. Working by instinct rather than mathematics, great leaders have achieved effects as sure and precise as if they had calculated each variable to the final decimal point.

Thus, Jesus set out confidently to convert the world by training only 12 apostles for a mere three years. Thus, Thomas Paine ignited a revolution by publishing a single pamphlet called *Common Sense*. Great leaders seem to know instinctively how to achieve massive results through minimal action. They seem to know just the *right actions* to perform at precisely the *right time.*

NETWORK MARKETING: THE HIDDEN ADVANTAGE

Of course, Sue Grigsby was neither a Jesus nor a Thomas Paine. She had no more special instinct for applying the Butterfly Effect than you or me. But she did have one key advantage. Sue had the extraordinary good fortune—and foresight—to have started building a network marketing business just three months before she was laid off from her job.

Network marketing—often called multilevel marketing, or MLM—refers to any method of marketing that allows independent sales representatives to recruit other sales representatives and to draw commissions from the sales of those recruits. The power of this technique lies in the fact that it enables you to acquire an organization, or "downline," of independent sales reps, or "distributors," who continue selling and recruiting long after you have retired from the business. You thus gain a *residual* income that keeps coming in whether or not you keep working.

Of course, it takes hard work and, in most cases, years of persistent effort to build such a large, self-sustaining downline. Many try and fail. But you don't need a huge downline to begin enjoying some of the key advantages of network marketing. A downline of *any size,* no matter how small or unprofitable, already places a unique power in your hands. It provides ordinary people like Sue Grigsby with an unusual ability to obtain massive results through minimal action.

A Change in Perspective

Like most people, Sue Grigsby knew almost nothing about network marketing. What little she had heard about the industry seemed mostly negative.

"Network marketing offended my sense of dignity," she recalls. "I thought it was something only desperate people did."

Sue Grigsby could afford to be smug in the days before her divorce. Her husband was a successful heating and cooling contractor, making $250,000 per year. Sue lived in a comfortable, custom-built home. She didn't have to work. Her whole attention was devoted to her house, her children, and her hobbies. Then, one day, the dream came crashing down. Afflicted by what Sue calls "midlife crisis," her husband suddenly sued for divorce.

"To say that I was in despair would be an understatement," Sue recalls. "I really wanted to die. I was 50 years old and all alone. I wanted my husband back, but he wasn't coming back. I was just heartsick."

Blood Money

With the house and furniture sold, Sue moved into a small apartment with her youngest son, then in his teens. Things were tough. But, after a few months, Sue managed to struggle to her feet, earning $60,000 a year working a sales territory for a major giftware company. The money was excellent. But Sue paid for it in blood.

"I was working 90 hours a week, like a machine," she says. "I was exhausted. I didn't have a private life."

Every morning, Sue loaded up her car with what felt like hundreds of pounds of catalogs and sample cases. Her sales territory covered a huge stretch of Connecticut countryside. At the end of the day, every joint of her body would ache from lifting and carrying. Her skin would break out from the stress. But for Sue, there was no escape. She needed this job to live. As the oldest person on the sales force, Sue could only hope and pray that her strength would hold out.

Burnout

Unfortunately, Sue's mental and physical endurance was already ebbing by the day. One afternoon, Sue found herself driving alone through a remote stretch of mountainous country on the way to her next sales call. Snow fell in wet clumps on the windshield. Every muscle in her body ached.

The car's heater could not drive the winter chill from her bones. That's when it hit her: blind, animal panic. "I had this overwhelming fear that I was going to die from all the pressures," says Sue. "I felt I was never going to have a family again, that I was going to lose my health, that I'd have to stop working, and I'd be all alone. Tears were just welling in my eyes. My whole body froze. Panic gripped me. I felt like I was in a vice."

Somehow, Sue managed to pull herself together and get through that day. But her time in the company was fast coming to a close. Though she feared to put it in words, Sue knew in her heart that she was *burning out*. And if she knew it, that meant her managers could sense it too.

Death of a Saleswoman

Burnout. It eventually happened to all the sales reps at Sue's company. That was taken for granted. From her first day on the job, Sue had noticed the haunted gaze of the veteran reps, the pallor of their skin, the sag of their shoulders. What she hadn't realized is how quickly it gets to you. Only three years on the job, and already it was Sue's eyes that now stared from the bathroom mirror each morning jaded, spent, and afraid. Each morning, when she heaved her sample cases into the trunk of her car, Sue found that she staggered just a bit more feebly beneath their weight, paused just a few seconds longer to catch her breath, shivered just a tad more stiffly in the chill New England breeze.

On that fateful morning, when, at last, Sue sat in the breakfast room of the Ramada Inn, listening to the hollow drone of her boss's words as if from a million miles away, something surprising and unfamiliar stirred in her heart. It was a feeling deeper than Sue's initial sense of shock at being laid off, deeper than her anger or fear, deeper even than her shame. So deeply buried was this feeling that it wasn't until after the meeting, when Sue got in her car and started home, that she finally succeeded in naming it. *Relief.* That's what she felt. Overwhelming relief. "I remember telling myself again and again, 'It's over,'" says Sue. "'It's finally over.' I remember thinking, 'Thank God, I don't have to go back there anymore. Now I can finally rest.'"

J.O.B. = Just Over Broke

When she got home, Sue brewed herself a cup of orange pekoe tea and sat quietly in her living room for a long time. Sue realized that her unemployment checks would only go so far. She would have to find another job, and soon. But every time Sue considered this prospect, she was overcome by an almost physical wave of revulsion.

"I couldn't do it," she recalls. "I just couldn't face writing another resumé."

Only now did Sue begin to realize how angry she really was. On a whim, this regional manager had snatched away her livelihood—and handed it to someone else! Her years of service, her sincerity, her dedication meant nothing to him. Sue realized that as long as she worked for others, she was only a cog in their machine, and a disposable one at that.

"It was humiliating to think that someone had taken control of my life that way," Sue recalls, "that someone had eliminated my options."

The truth is, Sue didn't want another job. What she wanted was a new life. And, as she sat on that couch, sipping her tea, it slowly began to dawn on Sue, for the very first time, that she might already have the means of getting what she wanted.

The Pest

"In network marketing," says Sue, "*no one* can take your territory away from you. It's yours for life."

Nine and a half years before, Sue had gotten an unexpected visit from an old friend. After years of absence, her friend—who now called himself "Showshawme"—had phoned her unexpectedly on New Year's Day.

"I'd like to come over," said Showshawme. "I have something very important to show you."

Sue had to grin with amusement. Showshawme hadn't changed a bit. Ever since she had known him, Showshawme had been a tireless huckster. He was *always* selling. In the time she'd known him, Showshawme had pushed bee pollen, pyramid power, and alfalfa sprouts grown in buckets in his bathtub, all with the same furious passion.

A bony little man with an impish gleam in his eye, Showshawme was afire with enthusiasm. When he was selling, Showshawme's beady eyes would glow like coals. He would pace up and down the room, waving his arms and jabbering like an auctioneer on five cups of coffee. Although he was forever declaring that someday he would be a millionaire, Showshawme never seemed to raise enough money even to take his car in for a new muffler or a badly needed paint job.

Still, he never gave up. Persistence was Showshawme's most notable trait. Even his friends referred to him half-jokingly as "the Pest." In fact, Sue was one of the few people with the patience and good humor to endure Showshawme's company for any length of time.

The Product

On that particular New Year's Day, Showshawme showed up at Sue's house—not surprisingly—with yet another unusual product to sell. This time, he was pushing little green capsules, which Showshawme said contained Super Blue Green Algae. This special breed of algae, Showshawme explained, grew only in a remote lake near Klamath Falls, Oregon. There, it was harvested for its unique nutritional properties by a company called Cell Tech—a network marketing company.

"He tried to recruit me into his downline," says Sue, "but I had no interest in building a Cell Tech business. Still, I did try the algae, and, to my surprise, it really did give me a charge. So I signed on as a distributor, just so I could buy the algae at the wholesale price."

For nine and a half years, Sue continued eating the algae every day. Her health improved in a number of ways. For the first time in years, Sue was able to get her weight under control. Her skin and hair took on a youthful glow. Her joints became limber. Her energy soared. Though she was pushing 50, Sue found that she looked and felt younger with each passing year. Nevertheless, she refused all of Showshawme's pleas to start working the business herself. Sue was happy just being a customer. Eventually, even the tireless Showshawme finally gave up and stopped calling. It was many years before Sue heard from him again.

Timing Is Everything

Network marketers like to say that "timing is everything." Certainly that proved the case with Sue. She had to go through a divorce and three years of a miserable life before changing her mind about Cell Tech.

In fact, it wasn't until three months before Sue's layoff that something finally happened to shake her complacency. Because she was enrolled as a Cell Tech distributor, Sue received the company newsletter. One day, as she flipped through the pages, Sue was startled to see an article about her old friend Showshawme. "The Pest" had gone on to become one of Cell Tech's top-ranking Double Diamond distributors! According to the article, Showshawme was now semiretired, spending most of his time pursuing self-improvement seminars and jetting off to exotic Caribbean islands. Showshawme had also become a philanthropist, contributing large sums of money to Cell Tech's charitable projects. Through it all, his five-figure income kept rolling in month after month, with little or no effort on Showshawme's part. (For more of Showshawme's story, see Chapter 6.)

"I couldn't believe it," says Sue. "All of a sudden, I had to ask myself, 'Where would I be now if I had been working the business all these years, like Showshawme?'"

The Seeds of Greatness

Sue did not have the slightest notion of how to go about starting an MLM business. As her sponsor—the person who recruited Sue into the business—Showshawme was responsible for training her. But he was out of town and unreachable by phone. Sue had no one to turn to.

Nevertheless, she got on the phone and started talking to friends about the algae. Sue's 90-hour-per-week sales job prevented her from spending much time on Cell Tech. But, by the time she was laid off, Sue had managed to acquire eight regular customers and a handful of occasional buyers.

Technically, Sue now had a downline of eight distributors—even though the "distributors" were nothing more than retail customers who had signed up in order to qualify for a wholesale discount. In fact, Sue was lucky if she could squeeze a few hundred bucks in commissions from her Cell Tech business each month. So where was all this incredible power that we have said Sue held in her hands? It lay, of course, in the Butterfly Effect.

YOUR COMPLEX DOWNLINE

Like the earth's atmosphere, an MLM downline is a *complex system.* In a typical downline, hundreds—even thousands—of human beings interact with each other in a billion unpredictable ways. That gives the Butterfly Effect plenty of leverage to do its work.

As with the weather, an MLM downline responds *massively* to the tiniest of stimuli. Successful network marketers have learned instinctively to stir up hurricanes of growth and sales in their downlines through the faintest flap of their "wings." The most subtle adjustment in your attitude, your style, your prospecting strategy, or your sales pitch can send your downline spinning off into an unstoppable whirlwind of success—or draining away in a dismal swirl of failure.

Obviously, it is imperative that you make the *right* adjustments. This book was written to help you do just that.

17,860 Relationships

But wait a minute. Remember that Sue Grigsby had only eight distributors in her downline. How complex can the interactions between eight people really be?

Far more complex than you think!

Mathematicians say that the number of personal relationships possible between a given group of people is equal to $1/2\,N\,(N-1)$, with N representing the number of people in the group. By this reckoning, there could be as many as 36 possible relationships between Sue and her eight distributors. But that's not all! Once they start working the business, each of the distributors in Sue's downline begins interacting with a small circle of friends and acquaintances—a Circle of Influence, in MLM parlance—in an attempt to sell them products or gain recruits. If we say that each distributor has frequent contact with 20 or so prospects (a very low estimate!), and include that Circle of Influence in our N figure, then N will equal 189—Sue, her eight distributors, and all 180 of their immediate prospects. Half of N equals approximately 95. Now take N minus one—or 188—and multiply it times 95. Our formula tells us that Sue's organization could easily yield 17,860 personal relationships, each with its own unique chemistry of inspiration, cooperation, and synergy. Now *that's* complexity!

Right Action, Right Time

Needless to say, Sue Grigsby knew nothing of such calculations as she sat on her couch that morning drinking her orange pekoe tea. She knew only that she was desperate—desperate enough to take an incredible risk. Sue took her desperation to bed with her that night. Perhaps she even dreamt of it. For when she awoke the next morning, Sue had already made a firm decision.

"I decided I wasn't going to get another job," says Sue. "I was going to go full-time in my Cell Tech business."

Sue's decision did not make the evening news. It was not debated in Congress, reported in the papers, or announced from church pulpits, nor was it heralded by a fanfare of golden trumpets. In fact, nobody really cared about Sue's decision at all, except Sue herself, her eight distributors, her three children, and her elderly mother (who was against it). Out of the millions of survival decisions made every day by tens of millions of out-of-work Americans, Sue's was just one more in the mix, a desperate gamble by a lonely, frightened woman in Windsor, Connecticut.

Nevertheless, that small decision proved to be just the *right action* at the *right time*. Like a wisp of air from a butterfly's wings, it whirled and spun and curlicued off into the void. Through the 17,860 relationships of Sue Grigsby's downline and prospect base, her decision echoed with inconceivable subtlety, working its way into voices that insisted with just a bit more passion that this algae *really works;* into hands that lifted the phone bravely off the hook for *just one more* cold call; into eyes that made infinitesimally sharper contact with prospects.

Who Knows?

Who can say, in the final analysis, where the effects of Sue's decision stopped and where other factors took over? We can no more draw clear lines in this matter than we could determine the effects of each tiny air current and temperature shift on a raging hurricane.

Yet, we can say that on the day Sue made her decision, Cell Tech had acquired only 30,000 distributors after ten full years in the business. Four years *after* Sue's decision, Cell Tech's downline had grown to 350,000—more than a tenfold increase.

As with the hurricane, there were, of course, myriad factors in Cell Tech's phenomenal growth. It was during those critical four years that the "Green Wave" hit in force—a nationwide obsession with healthy diet and herbal medicine. It was also during those years that Cell Tech introduced sleek new tools for its distributors, such as prospecting videos and audiotapes as well as highly effective sales scripts (see Chapter 6).

Nevertheless, Sue's impact was critical. When Sue phoned her downline and announced her decision to go full-time, four distributors out of the eight were so inspired that they resolved on the spot to start working the business themselves. Today, their ranks have grown to over 2,000. Then, when Sue finally reached Showshawme on the phone and told him the news, Showshawme got so excited about the idea of working with Sue to achieve her goals that he too announced that he was coming out of semiretirement and reentering the business full-time. Today, Showshawme's downline accounts for over *90 percent* of Cell Tech's 350,000 distributors—the vast majority of them recruited *after* Sue's decision.

The Dream

As of this writing, Sue earns close to $6,000 in commissions per month—comparable to what she used to make at her old company. Only now, Sue works from home and makes her own hours. She has time to spend with her granddaughter and her new boyfriend. And, most important for Sue, never again will anyone have the power to steal her "sales territory" and give it to someone else.

Critical Mass

"When it happens, it's like nothing you can imagine," says Sue. "For me, it hit about eight or nine months into the business. All of a sudden, it just exploded. My checks started doubling and tripling. That's when I realized the equation had started happening, the one they tell you about in the beginning but that you never quite believe."

Every network marketer knows what Sue means by "the equation." When you start out in the business, they tell you that if you work hard and persist, eventually your organization will hit "critical mass"—that magical point when just the right number of people, just the right level of enthusiasm, and just the right timing in the marketplace converge to ignite an explosion of "momentum" in your downline—MLM jargon for sudden, wild, exponential growth.

Unfortunately, few ever reach that mystical point. That's because it takes more than just hard work and persistence to get there. It takes the will and the judgment to make correct choices and to make them at the right time.

Sue Grigsby's decision to "burn the boats" was crucial in mobilizing her downline into action. But her efforts would have been wasted if she had followed that decision with ill-conceived and erroneous actions. The Butterfly Effect is always powerfully at work in your downline. But it works in your *favor* only when you steer it resolutely on the right course, day after day.

Maximize Your Leverage

No matter how small, your MLM downline places in your hands an incredible power—and an equally great responsibility. Make the right moves, and your efforts will be rewarded by lightning growth, thousands of times more intense than your expended effort. Make the *wrong* moves and . . . well, let's put it this way. Read the rest of this book, so you *don't* make the wrong moves!

For six years, I have conducted in-depth interviews with some of the top achievers in MLM, extracting from them success secrets known only to a few. These men and women are masters of the Butterfly Effect. Through the years, they've developed their own unique way of working the business, a way that employs minimal action to attain massive results. I call it the Wave Three Way.

You and your downline can also walk the Wave Three Way. In this book, you will find many of the most cherished secrets of the Butterfly Masters. These principles can turn your MLM organization into a magical lens through which your slightest efforts are magnified a thousandfold. Follow the Wave Three Way, and that bucking bronco you call your downline will transform into a magnificent steed, whose fearsome brawn will leap at your every command.

Chapter 2

THE WAVE-THREE EXPLOSION

Michael S. Clouse is a busy man. In addition to his job as editor-in-chief of *Upline,*—a leading trade publication for network marketers—Michael is also the father of two teenage children, a distributor for an MLM company called The Peoples Network (TPN), and a professional speaker with a full schedule of out-of-town engagements. Two to three times per month, Michael goes on the road. When he returns, he inevitably finds his home office in Seattle swamped with incoming messages.

"Typically, I'll find a stack of up to 20 messages regarding *Upline,*" says Michael. "In addition, I'll have a lot of catching up to do with my children, finding out what's going on in their lives and what school activities I'm supposed to attend."

The one thing Michael does *not* have to do when he comes back from a trip is to catch up with his network marketing business. That is the single area of his busy life that seems to take care of itself.

"When I got back from my last several business trips," says Michael, "there was not a single message that needed to be returned regarding my activities with TPN."

A Revolution

Michael runs his MLM business the Wave Three Way. He exploits telecommunications and "automated" selling techniques to cut his personal work time to a minimum. On those occasions when he must work on his TPN business, Michael leverages his time by exploiting the Butterfly Effect.

Since about 1990, millions of MLMers have embraced the Wave Three Way. An explosion of companies and distributors employing Wave-Three techniques has revolutionized the industry, transforming MLM from a tedious, low-status pursuit to a glistening model for 21st-century commerce—a model that is fast attracting the most talented and ambitious professionals in America.

WHAT IS "WAVE THREE"?

In my book *Wave Three: The New Era in Network Marketing* I suggested that the MLM industry was now entering its third and most powerful phase of evolution.

Wave One began in 1941, when a chemist named Carl Rehnborg introduced the first multilevel compensation plan into his company, Nutrilite Products, Inc. This was the wild and woolly stage of MLM, when legitimate companies competed neck and neck with outright pyramid scams, and neither the public nor the government were quite sure of the difference. Wave One ended in 1979, when the Federal Trade Commission ruled that Amway—and, by implication, network marketing itself—was a legitimate business.

Then came Wave Two. For the first time, PC technology made it cheap and easy to track the complex flow of commissions through an MLM downline. Armed with little more than a desktop computer and a homemade product line, entrepreneurs by the hundreds rushed to start their own network marketing companies from bedrooms and garages across America. The 1980s saw an unprecedented explosion of MLM startups.

The Part-Time Barrier

Wave Two also saw millions of people flocking to join MLM companies. Unfortunately, many left embittered by the experience. The problem was that the vast majority of network marketers are part-timers—people looking to earn only a few hundred dollars per month on the side. Part-timers are the backbone of any downline. You can't build a business without them.

Unfortunately, part-timers found it difficult to make money in Wave-Two companies. It was brutal, round-the-clock work. Distributors had to stockpile inventory, fill product orders, speak before crowds at hotel meetings, train new recruits, and stay up all night fielding calls from their downlines. Even worse, Wave-Two companies often practiced "frontloading"—compelling distributors to "qualify" for their commissions each month by purchasing huge quantities of inventory, most of which ended up collecting cobwebs in the distributor's garage.

User-Friendly Process

Wave-Three companies set out to change all that. Starting in about 1990, a new generation of CEOs began streamlining the network marketing process to make it more user-friendly. Their goal was to create a business opportunity in which *anyone* could make money, from the part-timer to the "heavy hitter."

Wave-Three companies use computers, sophisticated management strategies, and cutting-edge telecommunications to make life as easy as possible for the average distributor. Product orders are now fulfilled directly by the company instead of by the distributor. Prospecting is done via mass-mailed videotapes; creative Web sites; and cooperative advertising in which distributors split the costs of placing direct-response ads in major media. Three-way phone calls enable new distributors to listen in quietly while their more experienced sponsors conduct sales presentations. Fax-on-demand services provide up-to-the-minute information on products, prices, company activities, and policies, at the touch of a button on your telephone. Voice-mail and e-mail broadcasts allow leaders to communicate instantaneously with hundreds of downline distributors. Even the most inexperienced or tongue-tied distributor can now treat prospects to a professional sales presentation by dialing into a teleconference or turning on a satellite TV broadcast.

These are just a few of the techniques Wave-Three companies use to automate and standardize the once-onerous task of managing a downline. In addition, more and more companies are eliminating heavy "qualifiers" from their compensation plans, so part-timers are no longer pressured to invest more time and money than they can afford.

A 34 Percent Increase

Wave Three is still in its infancy. But, even at this early stage, its effects on the industry are apparent. According to *The Wall Street Journal,* the number of network marketers in the United States has risen from an estimated 2.3 million to 3.1 million independent distributors since 1990—an increase of 34 percent. The same article states that since 1993, the number of full-time MLMers has doubled. About one-fourth of all network marketers now work their businesses full-time.

THE NEW BREED

Michael S. Clouse typifies the new breed of MLM professional. He worked his way up the ladder of corporate America. In the 1980s, Michael headed the computer division for First Interstate Bank's leasing program. Later, he became a highly paid trainer and marketing consultant for AT&T. Then Michael caught the MLM dream. He joined his first network marketing company back in 1988, when Wave Two was still going strong. Michael suffered through many of the industry's worst growing pains. He came very close to leaving network marketing forever. But the Wave-Three Revolution brought Michael back. He learned that it was now possible to work an MLM business with the same professional efficiency to which he was accustomed in corporate America.

The Wave-Two Experience

As recently as 1991, Michael can remember spending hours on the phone with hundreds of downline distributors every time the head office made an announcement. If, for example, the company rolled out a new line of products, it might take up to two and a half months before the announcement appeared in its quarterly magazine. Michael wasn't willing to wait that long for his downline to place orders. He would have no choice but to convey the message himself.

"My wife and I would spend up to 20 minutes on the phone with each person in our downline," says Michael. "We would explain why we have this new product, where it came from, who's going to make it for us, when we're going to have it available for purchase, what the discounts are, why you need to order it now, the benefits for you, and the benefits for your group. In effect, we would conduct up to 200 individual sales presentations."

The Garbled Grapevine

Even then, announcements were constantly being garbled as they filtered through the grapevine. Calls would trickle in for days from distributors seeking clarification. Rumor control was a major part of Michael's job.

"My wife and I would return home to find 10 to 15 messages waiting," says Michael. "We would spend virtually every night of the week through the dinner hour and well into the evening returning calls. It was never-ending. We wound up with very large telephone bills."

Televised Briefings

Nowadays, Michael handles new product announcements a little differently—he doesn't handle them at all. His present company, TPN, takes care of that through its private satellite TV network. On most nights, TPN broadcasts self-help programming by such motivational gurus as Jim Rohn and Brian Tracy. But every Monday at 6 P.M., TPN distributors across the nation gather around their sets for an hour-and-a-half business briefing direct from company president Jeff Olson. When Olson goes on the air, every distributor in the company is guaranteed to be watching. The company provides free satellite dishes to each new recruit. (For more on TPN and Jeff Olson, see Chapter 11.)

During these televised briefings, every important aspect of the business is explained and reviewed: the compensation plan; the specials and promotions; the product line; conventions and training events—virtually every nettlesome detail that upline leaders were once expected to transmit by phone to their downlines.

Added Value

The benefits of satellite networking came home dramatically to Michael Clouse following a company announcement that it was adding a new "faculty" member—Og Mandino, world-renowned author of the motivational classic *The Greatest Salesman in the World.* One of TPN's most important products is its motivational programming. The announcement of a new program featuring Og Mandino would therefore add tremendous value to the TPN opportunity.

"In another company," says Michael, "it would have been the equivalent of offering a new health supplement or a new skin care item."

A skilled practitioner of the Butterfly Effect, Michael Clouse knew that the confidence and excitement generated by this single announcement could translate instantly into higher sales and higher recruitment rates. It was imperative not only to get the message out to his downline but to make sure the distributors understood exactly how to exploit this information in their prospecting.

Automated Leadership

Unfortunately, Michael was out of town on business when the announcement was made. Past experience with Wave-Two companies told Michael to brace himself for a barrage of phone queries, at least half of which would be from people asking, "Who's Og Mandino?"

But when Michael got home, he found that his job had already been done.

"I found a few e-mail messages saying, 'Isn't that great?'" Michael recalls. "I had one voice message saying, 'Unbelievable!' What I *didn't* have was one single person call me up and ask, 'What does it mean?' They all *knew* what it meant. It was very refreshing."

Every distributor in Michael's downline had been thoroughly briefed, via satellite. There was literally nothing left for Michael to do—other than sit back and enjoy the surge of commissions that the announcement was bound to stimulate.

BEYOND "HIGH TECH, HIGH TOUCH"

Futurist John Naisbitt predicted that people would compensate for the dehumanizing effects of "high tech" advances by becoming more "high touch"—friendlier, more sensitive, and more caring. Wave-Three network marketing goes beyond Naisbitt's prediction. By freeing people from drudgery, Wave-Three technology actively empowers distributors to devote more time and energy to interacting with other people. High touch is a natural by-product of Wave-Three automation—not a reaction against it.

"Before Wave Three," says Michael, "we had to work with our distributors on everything from explaining the compensation plan to educating them on the product. Today, we get to work with them on one area alone—becoming friends. Our whole focus is on building a personal relationship."

Belly to Belly

Some MLM purists have decried Wave-Three methods as cold and impersonal. "Network marketing is a belly-to-belly business!" they cry. A talking head on the TV or a prospecting video in the mail can never replace face-to-face selling, they declare.

But these critics miss the point. Thanks to Wave Three, MLM has become more "belly-to-belly" than ever. Only the tedious, robotic tasks have been automated.

Network marketers have been freed to deploy their time and energy toward the *real* work—the work of leadership. "I just returned from Breckenridge, Colorado," says Michael. "I spent four days up in the mountains, hanging out with my friends. Six months ago, I didn't know who these people were. Now, I have an open invitation from them to return to the beautiful Colorado Rockies anytime I choose. And, yes, we talked about business. But we also spent some time enjoying this thing we call living. They took us up to see the Continental Divide. I've never had that sort of experience in network marketing before."

Bonds of Trust

The bonds of trust and friendship that Michael builds with his distributors today will pay off in future years through increased retention rates, higher morale, and greater synergy throughout his downline. Like leaders in every age and endeavor, Michael deals principally with the soul. The rapport he has developed with his downline could never have been achieved by phoning every couple of weeks to harangue them about the latest company bulletin. Wave Three has brought dignity and peace to Michael's organization.

Food for the Soul

You are privileged, dear reader, to have entered network marketing on the eve of revolution. Never before have upline leaders possessed the leisure to focus so profoundly on the problems of human motivation. Here, in that glowing crucible we call human emotion, the Butterfly Effect works its magic. Master its secrets, and, like the wise old monarchs of yore, you will lead your kingdom—your downline, that is—to a better life.

Chapter 3

TURN DOWN THE PRESSURE

Jim Kossert used to wear down his prospects with the persistence of a pit bull. Every objection they raised, Jim answered. Every excuse they offered, he shot down. On prospecting calls, Jim would argue, wheedle, coax, cajole—even beg. The one thing he wouldn't do was take no for an answer. Many joined Jim's downline just to get him off their backs.

"I wanted it worse than most people did," says Jim. "So I would drag people into it and get them involved, whether they wanted to or not."

Despite all his prospecting success, Jim had one serious problem. His downline just wouldn't perform. Instead of business builders, Jim's organization was filled with quitters and complainers. Jim worked three different network marketing companies in seven years, but he never managed to achieve a consistent, full-time income.

LESS PRESSURE, BETTER RECRUITS

Things have changed for Jim Kossert. Today, he's an MLM superstar. In less than five years, Jim grew his downline from zero to 90,000 distributors, with personal earnings in excess of $200,000 per month. How did he do it?

Jim had a revelation. He discovered, one day, that when he *turned down the pressure,* he got more and better

29

recruits. This single adjustment in Jim's strategy turned his business around. It set off a Butterfly Effect that made him a multimillionaire within three years. Here is Jim's story.

Rebel Without a Cause

All his life, Jim Kossert had resisted getting a job. One year short of his accounting degree, he dropped out of college.

"I couldn't see myself sitting behind a desk working for somebody," he explains.

Jim worked as a commercial fisherman and a real estate broker. He tried several network marketing businesses. But nothing Jim tried seemed to bring him the freedom he craved.

By the age of 34, Jim Kossert was a desperate man. He had a $150,000 mortgage on his house. Though he worked like a dog seven days a week at his real estate business, Jim averaged only $3,000 to $7,000 per month, with wild swings in his income every time the economy shifted. With a wife and two children to support, Jim was feeling the pressure more and more with each passing day.

"I was run down," says Jim. "I was 40 pounds overweight. Given another five years, I was a heart attack waiting to happen."

Slave to the Beeper

Even worse was the toll on Jim's family life. In real estate, you must be ready, night or day, to jump at your client's command. Jim was a slave to his beeper. His wife and children hardly knew him.

"It was scaring me," he recalls. "It wasn't good for my marriage. I wanted out."

The last straw came when Jim's pager went off in the middle of a family birthday party. Jim flew out the door to show a house. When he returned, three hours later, the party was over.

"No one said anything," says Jim, "but I felt like crap. I made up my mind right then that I had to do something different."

A Glass Ceiling

In his heart, Jim knew that network marketing was his only way out. Three times, he had tried and failed. But Jim had gotten close enough for a taste. There were times when Jim's downline seemed poised for explosive growth. His commission checks would climb to $5,000, $6,000, $7,000 per month. But just as Jim began to feel the excitement mounting, his commissions would slink back down again. It was as if some thin glass ceiling stood between Jim and his goals.

Hard work alone would never breach that barrier, Jim realized. Like the Grail Castle of legend, it would open only to those who knew the secret. But what was that secret? Jim resolved to find out.

Critical Mass or Bust

Jim's plan was to find the perfect network marketing vehicle and commit himself 100 percent to making it work. An opportunity soon fell in his lap. A real estate broker named Tyler Little who shared Jim's office cubicle had lost 25 pounds. It turned out that Tyler was using a natural product his wife had given him.

"I tried the product," says Jim, "and I lost 22 pounds in a single month. My energy level skyrocketed. I felt better than I had in years."

That's when Jim's friend explained that the product was sold through network marketing. "When I heard that, my eyes lit up," said Jim. "I told Tyler he had no idea what we had our hands on."

The Perfect Vehicle

Jim knew he had a great product. But what about the company—Enrich International? Two of Jim's previous companies had gone bankrupt, leaving him high and dry. So Jim approached this one with caution.

"I didn't want to get involved with another network marketing failure," he explains.

This time, Jim did his homework. He flew out to Orem, Utah, and met personally with Ken Brailsford, the company president. Brailsford was an entrepreneurial genius who had already made a fortune as the first person to sell herbs in capsule form. Then, in 1985, he had bought an herbal nutrition company called Nature's Labs and changed its name to Enrich. Brailsford's 20 years of experience in the herbal business combined with Nature's Labs' turnkey network marketing operation seemed a good combination. The new company even had its own pharmaceutical manufacturing subsidiary.

Checklist for Success

Jim thought long and hard about his decision. He didn't want any doubts eating away at his confidence when he called on his first prospect. But the more he reviewed the evidence, the more persuasive it seemed.

Enrich appeared to have everything. It was a ground-floor startup, offering maximum opportunity for rapid growth. It sold consumable products, which ensured re-

peat sales, and it targeted an explosive, growth market—
the multibillion-dollar alternative health sector. Even its
compensation plan seemed tailor-made to allow both full-
time and part-time distributors to prosper.

In short, Jim could find no flaw in the program. By
the time he signed up, Jim was convinced beyond doubt
that Enrich was his perfect vehicle.

Back Against the Wall

Russian chessmaster Gary Kasparov once said that he
deliberately allows himself to get into desperate situa-
tions on the chessboard. When his position looks hopeless,
that's when his deepest mental resources are unleashed
and he drives through to victory.

Instinctively, Jim Kossert followed the same plan.
With only enough money in the bank to support his family for a few months, Jim cleaned out his desk at the real
estate office and went home. From now on, Enrich would
be his full-time occupation.

"I think anybody—no matter what their race, reli-
gion, background, education, or whatever—when you put
their back up against the wall, they'll perform," says Jim.
"I wanted to do it right. I didn't want to look back someday and think I'd done it halfheartedly."

Massive Action

Jim's plan was to pour all his strength into one superhuman burst of activity, sustaining it until mental and
physical exhaustion forced him to stop. He would work
hard *one time,* for a few months or a couple of years
at most, then decelerate and enjoy the fruits of residual
income.

"I knew I'd have to work fast," he says, "because, in sales, your strength gives out sooner when you work slower. I knew it would have to be a short-term effort, because no human being can sustain that kind of pressure year after year. Finally, it had to be *massive,* because this is a numbers game. If I talked to 200 to 300 people, I knew I'd get rejections, but I'd also find some superstars."

Saw Now, Sharpen Later

From his previous MLM experience, Jim knew that procrastination was the enemy of effective prospecting. Benjamin Franklin once said that if he had four hours to chop down a tree, he'd spend the first three hours sharpening his saw. That's good advice. But too many network marketers use it as an excuse for procrastination. They invent the most elaborate rituals and routines of preparation in order to put off actually picking up the phone and making cold calls.

Jim resolved to avoid every excuse and distraction. He started by setting up a home office devoid of frills.

"I set aside a room in my house with a phone and an answering machine. A couple months later, I bought a fax. Those were my only three tools."

For a filing system, Jim took 12 manila envelopes and labeled them "January" through "December." Anything that had to do with Enrich went in the folder for that month, from lunch receipts to check stubs.

"At tax time, I just handed the folders to my accountant and said, 'You figure it out.' I didn't want to get bogged down with trivial stuff. I knew what I did best was talk on the telephone. If it wasn't ringing, I was making calls. Other stuff, like going to the post office to send out information packets to prospects, you do that in your down time. That stuff doesn't count. It's nonproductive."

From Warm List to Warm List

To get his leads, Jim drew up a "warm list"—a roster of 375 friends, acquaintances, and work associates. Then he started calling. From each new recruit, he obtained a new warm list. Then he would call each prospect on the new warm list, often in a three-way conference call with the recruit who had provided the list.

In this way, Jim worked from one warm list to the next and never seemed to run out of leads. Later, he also placed advertisements in the local newspaper.

A Subtle Change

In Jim's mind, the power of his strategy lay in the sheer volume of prospects he could reach by phone. For 16 hours per day, seven days a week, Jim's ear was glued to the receiver. He competed with himself to see how many people he could squeeze into a single hour. Eventually, Jim honed his pitch down to ten minutes, allowing him to prospect six people an hour, as many as 60 to 100 per day.

Jim's heroic pace was admirable. It gave him enormous leverage in building his downline. Nevertheless, it wasn't the critical factor in his success. Many network marketers have achieved comparable results with a far less punishing regimen.

The real catalyst in igniting Jim's fiery growth was neither his speed nor his numbers. It was a subtle change in his selling style that came about not through conscious decision but as a by-product of Jim's ferocious speed. Subtle as it was, the change proved fateful. It set in motion a Butterfly Effect that transformed Jim Kossert into a very wealthy man.

Straight Shootin'

In his effort to squeeze 60 to 100 prospecting calls into a single day, Jim quickly discovered that he had no time for coyness. He had to get right to the point and get off the phone as quickly as possible. Many prospectors will beat around the bush and try to avoid as long as possible admitting that they are network marketers. They do this on the assumption that the words "network marketing" will turn people off. Jim had no time for such niceties, however. He had a schedule to keep. This worked in Jim's favor in some unexpected ways.

His pitch went something like this: "Hi, this is Jim Kossert. I'm involved with a company called Enrich. I'm in network marketing and we've got some great products that flat-out work. Do you want to try them? Do you want to take a look at this opportunity?"

To Jim's surprise, about 10 percent of the people said yes, on the spot. This happened for three reasons:

1. *A high proportion of people today already know what network marketing is,* have a positive view of the industry, *and* have a need or desire for additional income.

2. *Jim's straightforward approach inspired trust and respect.* Because he did not try to conceal or downplay the fact that he was recruiting for an MLM company, prospects could see right away that Jim believed in his company and in his industry. They could also see that he wasn't the type who would deceive or bamboozle them.

3. *Jim was asking only for a limited commitment.* He did not ask his prospects to sign up on the spot. He asked only if they would try the product or if they would like more information about the opportunity.

The Four Big Objections

But what about the other 90 percent of Jim's prospects? Most of them offered one of the Four Big Objections to network marketing:

1. "I tried network marketing, and it doesn't work."
2. "I don't have time."
3. "It's an illegal pyramid scheme."
4. "It's just not for me." (And its close variant, "I'm not a salesman type.")

In years past, Jim would have wasted precious minutes on the phone haggling with these people. But now he didn't have time. Jim knew from experience they would be poor prospects, in any case. Even if he could persuade some to join, they would most likely hurt rather than help his business.

"A person convinced against his will is of the same opinion still," says Jim, quoting MLM sales guru Mark Yarnell. "Even if you do manage to get these people involved, their belief system won't be there and they'll do poorly in the business. Then they'll start blaming the company, the products, the marketing plan, the industry, and everybody else but themselves. I didn't want a bunch of negative people running around telling everybody why it doesn't work.

"So when people said they weren't interested, all I said was, 'I appreciate your taking a couple minutes of your time. Good-bye.' Then I hung up and moved on."

Let Them off the Hook

Jim realized that a large percentage of prospects would say "yes" just to get him off the phone. This too wasted time and money. It forced Jim to send information packets to people who weren't interested. It also put him through a runaround of calling people back and setting

up face-to-face meetings that never happened or that
proved fruitless.

About two months into his business, Jim tried something new. When he gave his pitch, he followed it with the
words: "If you don't want to get involved, tell me now. It's
okay. It makes no difference to me whether you say yes
or no."

It turned out that a surprising number of people felt
they needed just this sort of permission to say no. By taking away their fear of offending him, Jim freed his
prospects to speak honestly. He saved enormously in time
and effort. As Jim puts it: "You might as well find out in
two minutes, versus two weeks later."

Disqualify 'em

Jim soon realized that he had evolved a completely new
way of prospecting. He called it *disqualifying*. Instead of
screening for the best prospects, you focus on eliminating
the worst ones.

Dealing with rejection is one of the most discouraging
of all experiences in network marketing. The more you
argue with prospects, the more they object, and the worse
you feel. In the twinkling of an eye, Jim had turned the
tables completely. Never again would he suffer rejection.
Now it was Jim who did the rejecting.

The Takeaway

This subtle shift in emphasis tipped the power scales dramatically in Jim's favor. When he spoke with prospects
now, his confidence crackled like an electric charge. Instinctively, prospects sensed Jim's power and were drawn
to it.

In fact, Jim got some of his best recruits by rejecting them. Many would call right back after he hung up the phone. In face-to-face meetings, when prospects raised objections, Jim would calmly pick up his notebook, thank them for their time, shake their hand, and start walking. Often, after a few seconds' pause to recover from their shock, they would cry out, "Hey, wait a minute! Come back here!"

Jim Kossert wasn't playing games. When he got up to leave, he really meant it. But his abruptness had the same effect as a Takeaway—one of the oldest tricks in sales. When you offer a product and then withdraw your offer, it tends to arouse a fear of loss in your prospect. Although he never planned it that way, Jim's unwillingness to argue with prospects gave him a crucial psychological advantage.

Give Them Room

Disqualifying prospects had another curious side effect on their behavior, Jim noticed. In many cases, as soon as they realized that Jim really didn't care whether they said yes or no, many prospects would let down their guard and start talking. It was as if Jim had given them room to be themselves. Prospects were then far more likely to answer personal questions and open up about their lives. This placed a powerful prospecting advantage in Jim's hands, which he exploited to the hilt.

BIG PURCHASE, BIG RISK

International sales consultant Neil Rackham and his colleagues at Huthwaite, Inc. spent ten years analyzing over

35,000 sales transactions. They discovered that the traditional closing, probing, and objection-handling techniques—while effective in small sales—were actually harmful when used on major corporate customers.

The reason for this, as Rackham explains in his book *SPIN Selling,* is that big sales involve *heavy risk* for the buyer. If a company executive buys a faulty computer system, he not only wastes money but loses status in the company. In addition, high-ticket sales usually include long-term contracts for service and support. If the relationship between buyer and seller goes sour, the buyer risks years of unpleasant interactions from which he cannot escape.

Big Needs, Big Sales

For this reason, sales professionals have learned that high-pressure tactics don't work in major sales. The risk your prospect perceives is real. It cannot be talked away. Therefore, the only way to close a major sale is to convince your prospect that he runs a *bigger* risk by *not* buying your product.

This is done by skillful questioning. You won't get anywhere by *telling* your prospect he's in trouble. You must lead him to draw this conclusion himself. Ask your prospect about his business problems. Then ask what other problems are created by those problems. Keep going until your prospect begins to realize *on his own* that his problems have much bigger implications than he ever suspected. That's when you swoop in to offer your product as the solution.

Neil Rackham and his team designed a revolutionary new method of selling based upon just this sort of skillful, patient probing. Called "SPIN selling," the strategy sparked an impressive Butterfly Effect among Rackham's Fortune 500 clients, several of whom experienced sales gains ranging from 27 percent to 76 percent in test groups using the new method.

MLM Prospects Are "Big" Customers

So what does this have to do with network marketing? In fact, MLM prospects share many psychological features with major corporate buyers. The decision to join a network marketing company is, after all, quite a big one. Like the corporate executive, an MLM prospect incurs heavy risk when he commits to your opportunity. He risks years of time and labor. He puts his reputation on the line before friends, family, and colleagues. And he must commit to a long-term relationship. As with the corporate executive, sales pressure and closing tactics will only insult his intelligence and drive him away. What he really needs is to be convinced that the risks of *not* joining your company greatly outweigh the risks of joining it.

As Jim Kossert discovered, this can be accomplished very quickly, once you understand the goal.

Skillful Probing

After disqualifying the doubters and the naysayers, Jim would ask each remaining prospect if he wanted more information about the opportunity. If the answer was yes, Jim would respond: "Before I send you anything, I need to know a little bit about you."

He would then subject each prospect to a barrage of questions designed to narrow the field even further. If a prospect had no patience for the questions, Jim concluded that he was not really interested. If the prospect answered the questions, however, the questions themselves would force the prospect to reflect on his financial situation and his reasons for investigating network marketing.

"I would say things like, 'Why did you respond to the ad?' 'What are you doing now?' 'What did you do before?' 'Where do you live?' 'Where did you live before?' 'Are you married?' 'What's your commitment to this thing? I only work with committed people.'"

Fears and Insecurities

Jim found that, once he gave people room to talk, they would open up quickly about their needs, fears, and insecurities. The very condition of our society ensures that most MLM prospects are already primed to perceive a big need for residual income.

"People out there are scared," says Jim. "Once I get them loosened up, prospects just come right out and tell me they don't have a retirement plan. They don't have savings. They don't know how they're going to pay for their kids' college education. They don't know if, in twelve months, they're going to be able to make their mortgage payment.

"People are looking at network marketing now, because what they thought worked in the past doesn't work anymore—corporate America. I can ask people, 'Are you *sure* you've got a secure job? Do you *really* know what you're going to be doing in five years?' They can't answer that question."

A Winning Strategy

Unlike his prospects, Jim can now answer such questions with ease and confidence. He has achieved a degree of financial freedom unimaginable to most Americans.

"It didn't really hit me until the sixth month," Jim recalls. "Up till then, I was just so focused on phone calls and three-way calls and conference calls that it never sank in what was happening."

That month, Jim got a check in the mail for $38,000. The next month, it was $42,000. Six months later, it was $70,000.

"All of a sudden, I found myself thinking, 'Wow, this is a lot of money,'" says Jim. "My organization was growing deeper and deeper, all on its own. I was getting calls from people all over the country who I didn't even know saying they were in my downline. That's when I started to realize this thing was bigger than I thought. I saw it had the potential of just going crazy."

Today, after five years, Jim no longer puts in 16-hour days. But he still works his business and works it hard.

"A lot of people in the business, when they reach a certain level of success, they just sit back and take it easy," says Jim. "They think they've arrived. But, for me, this is the time to switch into overdrive. Last month, I saw an 18 percent increase in my commissions. This month, it increased another 15 percent. Sure, I love fishing and playing golf. But you can't do that 24 hours a day."

A Chain Reaction

The Jim Kossert who made millions through Enrich International was no different from the rebellious youth who once dropped out of college because he didn't want to take orders and sit behind a desk. The obsessive spirit that drove Jim to make 100 prospecting calls per day was the same that once caused him to waste time arguing with prospects or to dash out of family birthday parties in quest of a sale.

In fact, Jim's restless energy and stubborn spirit were tremendous assets. But until Jim learned to harness them, they did more harm than good. It was a very subtle change that turned Jim's life around—but a change with massive consequences. By easing off on the sales pressure, Jim put the Butterfly Effect to work for him.

"It's a chain reaction," says Jim. "When you stop selling and start disqualifying, you feel better about yourself. The better you feel, the better you do in your business. I finally realized that I don't have to convince people to join my organization. I just have to stand tall and believe in what I'm doing. That, in itself, is enough to blow people's minds."

Chapter 4

KEEP IT SIMPLE

The man had listened attentively all through Marc Barrett's presentation. He had nodded at all the right places, asked appropriate questions, and maintained good eye contact. For two whole hours, Marc detected no sign of boredom or impatience. The man never so much as twitched in discomfort. *This is the one,* thought Marc. *My first recruit.*

"Well," said Marc at the end, nearly smacking his lips with anticipation. "What do you think?"

"It looks great," said the man. "But I guess it's not for me."

Marc's smile froze on his face.

"Oh, uh . . . really?" Marc managed to say through his teeth. "Why is that?"

The man shrugged. "I can see you really know your stuff," he said. "You're obviously going to be very successful at this business. But I don't think it would work for me. It's too hard."

Long after the prospect left, Marc sat in his conference room staring at the empty chairs. For the first time since starting his NuSkin business, Marc began to wonder if he really had what it takes. A sense of panic began to steal over him. *Four months in this business,* he thought, *and I still haven't recruited my first distributor!*

A Different Kind of Sales

Marc had worked in sales all his adult life. He was good at it. Real good. Marc cleared his first million by age 28. By the time he turned 37, Marc had made—and lost—nearly $4 million in the real estate business.

But now, for the first time in his life, Marc found himself up against a sale that he just couldn't close. Marc couldn't understand it. He'd done everything right. He'd dazzled his prospects with two-hour presentations, bombarded them with facts and figures, awed them with his professional office in the Denver suburbs, impressed them with his stylish three-piece suits. In short, Marc had conducted each presentation with the polish and panache he might have used if he were pitching to the CEO of AT&T on a multimillion-dollar deal. Yet, not a single prospect had signed up.

What Marc failed to realize is that his perfectionism was his worst enemy. In network marketing, *simplicity*—not professional polish—is the best draw. Marc eventually got it straight. When he did, he not only turned his business around but went on to build a $30-million sales organization with NuSkin/IDN.

In Quest of Leverage

All his life, Marc Barrett had dreamed of achieving financial freedom. In college, he decided that one of his chief goals in life would be to buy a very large sailboat and sail around the world.

"I wanted to have time to do the things I really wanted to do," says Marc. "Free time was one of my major hot buttons."

Marc knew what he needed was leverage—a way to earn large sums of money with minimal effort. But how would he get it? One day in college, while lounging by a swimming pool in Miami, Marc allowed his gaze to wander up toward the high-rise apartment buildings nearby. *That's it,* Marc thought to himself. *That's the kind of leverage I need. If I owned buildings like that, I could just sit back and collect rent every month from each one of those apartments.*

It was a powerful vision. Marc was sure he had found the secret to financial leverage. But his plan would soon lead to the keenest disappointment of Marc's life.

Trouble in Paradise

Marc went on to make a fortune in real estate. By age 36, he was personally worth $3.8 million, most of it invested in 14 apartment projects in Denver. But the freedom Marc craved was still out of reach.

"I was a slave to my business," says Marc. "The more successful I became, the more projects I had to manage. If I wasn't out there producing and bringing new projects on line, there was no cash flow."

The Bubble Bursts

But Marc's harshest lesson was yet to come. When the oil business collapsed in the early 1980s, it set off a chain reaction through the Denver real estate market. The office buildings went first. Then the commercial and retail markets followed. Finally, as unemployment in Denver skyrocketed to 10 percent, residential real estate went through the floor. Marc suffered vacancy rates of up to 50 percent in some of his buildings.

Although a multimillionaire on paper, Marc had tied up virtually all his assets in his apartment projects. In a desperate attempt to stave off bankruptcy, Marc poured what little cash he had left into his buildings. But it was

all in vain. At age 37, Marc was ruined. He lost his buildings, his money, and, finally, his house. With money bor-
rowed from his mother, Marc moved his family into a
rented home. He was back where he had started 20 years
before. Except now, Marc had a wife and three children to
support.

"I'd always had faith in myself," says Marc. "But now
I started wondering if my past success had been one of
those lucky things, like winning the lottery. I started having real doubts about my ability to get it back."

Unemployable

In desperation, Marc did something he'd sworn he would
never do—he typed up a resumé and went looking for a
job. But Marc quickly discovered that successful entrepreneurs are virtually unemployable.

"I made employers nervous," he says. "They were
afraid they'd hire me and then, six months later, there'd
be a company that looked just like theirs next door."

While Marc scrambled to concoct some entrepreneurial scheme, his wife, Laura, quietly took matters into her
own hands. Laura had not worked for years. But, with a
sure instinct, she seized upon an opportunity that seemed
to offer everything she and her husband needed—ready
cash, self-employment, and long-term earning potential
in the millions.

A Second Chance

An old friend of Laura's named Connie Buetow recruited
her into a network marketing business—called NuSkin
International—that sold high-quality skin care products.

"She understood the potential right away," says Marc.
"She was really excited about it. She wanted us both to
do it."

But Marc wouldn't listen. In his mind, network marketing was a scam.

"I was convinced that she had been duped," he says. "As she got more involved, I started looking over her shoulder and examining the materials, because I didn't want her to get mixed up in something illegal."

Double Take

But the longer Marc looked, the more intrigued he became. He noticed, first of all, that his wife loved the products and seemed to have no trouble selling them.

NuSkin founder Blake Roney had discovered that the big-name skin care companies diluted their products with massive quantities of filler, such as beeswax and mineral oil. Some of them even added harsh chemicals that damaged or aged skin, while skimping on beneficial ingredients, such as vitamin E and aloe. Roney invented a new skin cream that consisted only of active, beneficial ingredients and that used no harmful substances. The "experts" told Roney his formula was too costly to manufacture and would soon drive him out of business. But NuSkin went on to become one of the great success stories of the 1980s, clearing half a billion dollars in annual sales by 1990.

All of that still lay in the future. What Marc saw in the late '80s was a great product, a growing company, and a marketing system that worked.

"I started seeing the potential for leverage," says Marc. "I saw people selling products, recruiting distributors, and having the potential to develop income streams of several hundred thousand dollars a year."

The Wave-Two Dilemma

Unfortunately, network marketing was still in its Wave-Two phase. Like most MLM companies at the time,

NuSkin provided little guidance for its distributors. You were pretty much on your own to develop a sales strategy. Marc and Laura quickly disagreed on their approach. By the time Marc joined, Laura had already reached the "executive" level in NuSkin's commission structure, so she insisted that Marc follow her successful example. But Laura's strategy was to set up beauty salon owners as distributors. Marc felt uncomfortable walking into salons and doing facial demonstrations. He also suspected there was better money elsewhere.

"I've always been in charge of my own business," says Marc. "I like to do things my way."

Eventually they came to an impasse, and Laura quit in frustration.

"She just said, 'Fine, you do it yourself, then,'" says Marc. "Laura had her hands full with the kids anyway, so we agreed that I would work the business on my own."

Procrastination

Marc soon ended up with egg on his face. He didn't have the slightest idea how to proceed. He couldn't even manage to duplicate Laura's previous level of success. So Marc did the next best thing—procrastinate.

Marc was still renting a $500-per-month office from his real estate business. Day after day, he would put on a suit and tie, go to his office, and putter around. Most of his time was spent on "due diligence," researching the industry and arming himself with facts. Marc rationalized that he would need these facts to overcome objections when he started selling. But his research soon became an endless excuse for doing nothing.

Rejection

When he couldn't procrastinate any longer, Marc made a few tentative calls on his old real estate chums. Some of them laughed outright. Others asked, jokingly, when he expected to get his first pink Cadillac. A few seemed genuinely concerned about Marc's sanity. "They would give me this funny look and ask how I was feeling," says Marc. "They figured the strain of my bankruptcy had finally pushed me over the edge." Run-ins like that would send Marc scurrying back to the safety of his "due diligence." But Marc knew he couldn't procrastinate forever. His continued dabblings in real estate were going nowhere. Both his wife and mother began hinting that it was time for Marc to get a job.

The Puzzle

"I'm very persistent," says Marc. "Once I decide I want to do something, it becomes a challenge to figure it out. It's like putting together a puzzle."

Marc knew there was a way to make this business work. He just had to solve the puzzle. Marc began looking around for successful NuSkin distributors who could teach him. Rumor had it that a guy named Marc Yarnell out of Austin, Texas, had signed up 30 people in his first month and cleared $15,000 in commissions by his fourth month in the business. Now Yarnell's monthly commissions were reputed to be four times that amount. Yarnell was directly upline from Marc, so he had an immediate financial interest in seeing that Marc did well in the business. Marc decided to give him a call.

Ask the Right Question

Unfortunately, you can't get the right answer until you ask the right question. Marc's pride still prevented him from seeking the kind of comprehensive help he needed. Marc saw himself as an expert on sales and marketing. He never imagined that there could be anything fundamentally wrong with his understanding of how the business worked. So, when he first spoke to Yarnell, Marc had a limited agenda. "In my mind, the problem was that my former real estate colleagues were not good prospects," says Marc. "I figured I needed a new source of prospects."

Marc found just what he was looking for—and no more. Although Yarnell explained very thoroughly the basics of the business, most of it went in one ear and out the other. The only part that Marc retained was Yarnell's advice to take out ads in local newspapers.

"Advertising made sense to me," says Marc. "It fit into my preconceived notions about how to do marketing."

A Partial Solution Is No Solution

In fact, Marc had only part of the solution. At first, Marc was delighted when his phone started ringing with eager new prospects. Advertising was the key!

But it quickly became clear that something was wrong. Marc would bring his prospects into the office, one after another, and dazzle them with facts and figures. They would listen politely through the whole two-hour presentation, shake Marc's hand at the end, and leave. Not a single one joined Marc's downline.

Duplicatability

A few weeks later, Marc was back on the phone with Yarnell.

"This time he did troubleshooting," says Marc. "He asked questions, kind of walking me through what I was doing."

At the end, Yarnell pronounced his verdict.

"You're not duplicatable," he said.

Duplicatable? thought Marc. This was not a familiar word. Marc remembered vaguely that Yarnell had mentioned something about "duplicatability" the last time they spoke. But Marc had ignored that part. It wasn't standard sales and marketing terminology, so Marc figured it must not be important.

"When you're giving someone a presentation," Yarnell continued, "they're looking at the business, but they're also looking at how you're doing the business. As they're watching the process, they're saying inside their heads, 'Can I do what he's doing?'"

In the case of Marc's prospects, the answer was no. They took one look at Marc's fancy office, his business suit, and his polished presentation and concluded that they couldn't *duplicate* it. Marc's approach seemed too expensive and too difficult.

Keep It Simple

Yarnell told Marc he needed to simplify his approach. He suggested three specific changes. First, Marc should stop giving his own presentations and use a prospecting video. Second, he should dress casually. Yarnell, for example, gave his presentations in a sport coat and a pair of blue jeans. Finally, Yarnell told Marc to lose the office.

"While you're talking," said Yarnell, "your prospects are looking around and saying, 'You mean I've got to get an office? Forget it!'"

A Humbling Experience

When Marc hung up the phone, he was in a state of shock. For the first time since starting his NuSkin business, he began to realize that he had a great deal to learn. But he was also truly open, for the first time, to learning it.

"The office was the hardest habit to break," says Marc. "In those days, working out of your home was still considered unprofessional. It implied that you couldn't afford an office. But I finally did it."

To Marc's surprise, he started winning recruits. The video he used had been produced by Yarnell himself. Prospecting videos were still a novelty in the late 1980s. But it worked like a charm.

"Even though I had excellent presentation skills," says Marc, "I followed Yarnell's advice and didn't even attempt to give my own pitch. I would just sit people down, plug in the videotape, and let them watch it."

After one such presentation, Marc's prospect—a CPA—turned to him and said, "I just want to know one thing. Can I get that tape and can I do what you're doing?"

Marc Barrett was in business.

Get Radical

Yet, Marc's results were still less than stellar. His recruitment was slow and his cash flow unimpressive. Marc knew there were still some pieces missing from the puzzle. But he didn't yet know where to find them.

Fate intervened. The house Marc had been renting outside of Denver was suddenly sold. Marc and his family had to move out. By now, Marc had given up trying to revive his real estate business. No more ties bound him to the Denver area. That's when a reckless idea began to germinate in his mind.

"Put all your eggs in one basket," said steel magnate Andrew Carnegie, "and watch that basket."

Until now, Marc realized, he had been pursuing his NuSkin business halfheartedly. He had only half listened to Yarnell. He had continued dabbling in real estate, devoting only a few hours each day to NuSkin. But now Marc sensed he was close to his goal. The jigsaw puzzle was nearly complete. Marc's NuSkin business was primed to take off. Maybe now was the time to get radical, Marc thought.

Marc knew that a major NuSkin convention was coming up soon in San Diego. There, Marc could meet and talk with many successful distributors. If there was any place on earth he was likely to find the missing pieces of the puzzle, it would be there.

"We made the decision then to put all of our stuff in storage," says Marc, "to go to San Diego, rent a house on the beach, sit there for a month, and go to the convention."

A LOT OF PEOPLE DOING A LITTLE

San Diego proved to be Marc's turning point. It was there that he met Jerry Campesi, a highly successful NuSkin distributor with 20 years' experience as a franchise consultant.

"Jerry had a real business background," says Marc. "He was able to explain the mechanics of network marketing in a way that finally made sense to me."

What Marc realized was that he had failed to understand the *objective* of a network marketing business.

"In my mind, the goal was to recruit 12 top-notch salespeople and train them to a high level of proficiency, just as I would do if I were setting up a real estate office," says Marc, "until eventually they were each moving $30,000 to $40,000 worth of product per month."

Campesi told Marc he was working the business *backward*. Only a highly trained and motivated salesperson could move $40,000 worth of product each month. But 100 ordinary people could easily sell that amount simply by consuming $400 worth, between themselves and a few friends, every month. The goal, in other words, was to get *a whole lot of people* doing *a small amount* of sales volume.

Sorting and Sifting

This led to Campesi's next point: Marc was spending far too much time trying to close each prospect.

"Again, it was my real estate background getting in the way," says Marc.

Marc knew that in Denver there might be only 5,000 people looking to buy a home at any one time. But there would be at least 30,000 real estate agents chasing them around trying to sell them one. That meant a lot of competition for a small target market. Any agent lucky enough to find a real, live prospect would use every trick in the book to pressure that prospect into a sale.

In network marketing, however, the opposite situation prevails. Virtually anyone who wants to earn extra money is a prospect—at least 50 percent of the population, according to Marc's estimate. So there's no need to waste time trying to sell any one person on the business.

"Campesi helped me understand that what we're really doing is promotional marketing—the art of putting information in front of people. You want to move quickly through the population, sifting and sorting, until you find people who are open to the opportunity."

The Irrelevant Three Percent

Would Campesi's advice really turn his business around? Marc wasn't sure. But Marc had grown to the point where he was finally willing to try something, even if he didn't understand it. Marc started sifting and sorting.

"I would give people a presentation, and, if they weren't interested, I went on to the next person. *Next* became my favorite word."

Immediately, Marc experienced a revelation. Because his own view of network marketing had been so negative, at first, Marc had assumed that all his prospects would hold equally negative views. But once he started sifting and sorting, Marc found that serious objections were rare. "I found that only 3 percent of the market had a truly negative perception of network marketing," he says. The rest, Marc discovered, were either positive toward the industry, neutral toward it, or had never even heard of it. With numbers like those, it was clearly a waste of time trying to persuade the negative 3 percent! Marc's presentation became less defensive and more instructional. He also started having more fun. Until he stopped doing it, Marc hadn't realized how much of his time, energy, and enthusiasm had been wasted fending off objections.

Total Absorption

For the first time, Marc found himself completely absorbed in building his downline. He hadn't focused so intently on any project since losing his real estate business. Hours would pass like minutes. At the end of a 16-hour day, Marc would find himself chomping at the bit to start over again the next morning. He had entered that state of profound mental absorption that psychologists call "flow"—that high-performance mind-set in which composers write great symphonies, athletes break records, and scientists devise breakthrough theories.

Marc's self-consciousness fell away like dry scales. He no longer worried about looking "professional." Marc invited prospects by the score to his ramshackle beach house.

"It was a little three-bedroom place," says Marc. "My office was in my daughter's bedroom. I did presentations in the living room. My wife would have to take the kids to go out to the beach or hide in the back part of the house."

Massive Results

At last, the final piece had fallen into place. Marc experienced a Butterfly Effect beyond every expectation. True to Campesi's word, Marc built up a huge volume without any one distributor having to carry the load.

"In the last year," says Marc, "I personally sold about $5,000 worth of product for the whole year, which is about $300 to $400 a month. But my business organization has generated anywhere from $10 million to $30 million per year, over the last three years."

Marc chooses not to divulge his personal earnings. However, he notes that he has attained the status of a Hawaiian Blue Diamond—an achievement level that implies average earnings of $700,000 per year.

The Learning Curve

Thanks to Marc Barrett's monumental pride, his learning curve was longer than most. But it wasn't all Marc's fault. He had the misfortune of trying to learn network marketing during the Wave-Two era, when sales tools and training techniques were primitive and inconsistent.

No one today would have to go through such a heroic quest to learn the basics of MLM. They would imbibe the core principles through three-way prospecting calls with their sponsors, satellite broadcasts, and multimedia training programs.

NuSkin, in particular—along with its health and nutrition subsidiary IDN—has gone on to become a leader in the Wave-Three Revolution. Its distributors today exploit a powerful infrastructure of telecommunications, automated product fulfillment, Internet Web sites, and a wide variety of prospecting videos and audiotapes—many produced by Marc Barrett himself—that help standardize the business and make it more duplicatable.

People Power

More than anything else, Marc Barrett has learned that it takes all levels of distributors to make a Wave-Three company run—from the business-builders who provide leadership, to the part-timers and wholesale buyers whose monthly purchases ensure a steady sales volume.

"Only about 1 percent to 5 percent of your recruits will look at it as a dead serious business," he concludes. "Forty-five percent are people with lower financial goals. They'll do a little retailing, make a few hundred dollars, recruit a few people, and that's it. The rest are people who come in as distributors so they can buy at wholesale."

In a conventional sales force, a mix like that would spell disaster. But, thanks to the magic of duplication, ambitious souls like Marc Barrett can build multimillion-dollar businesses, in large part, from the modest efforts of ordinary people.

Chapter 5

TELL A STORY

Emma Lyman was out of her league and she knew it. The man on the other end of the phone was a sophisticated businessman from California, while Emma had spent her whole adult life as a wife and mother, in Kansas City, Missouri ("the heart of America," as Emma likes to call it). Until she was nearly 60, the only work experience Emma had had was 40 years of teaching Sunday school. The only traveling she'd done had been driving back and forth from the grocery store and carting her six children between school, church, and music lessons.

Even so, Emma was nobody's fool. She knew when someone was talking down to her, and this gentleman from California was definitely doing it.

"I could sense this pious attitude behind his questions," says Emma, "as if he knew it all and I didn't."

Although he had answered one of Emma's recruitment ads in a magazine, the man seemed determined to talk himself out of joining Emma's downline. He just couldn't seem to believe that a woman like Emma could really be as successful as she claimed, and he seemed determined to find the catch. Every time Emma answered one of his questions, the man fired another at her, exploring the minutiae of her company's compensation plan as if he were a dentist probing for cavities.

Be Yourself

The more Emma talked to this man, the more pressure she felt to be someone different from who she really was. But Emma was too old to yield to that kind of pressure. She had spent her whole adult life in Kansas City and raised six children there. Everyone in Emma's world knew all her business, and she knew theirs. That didn't leave much room for pretense or play-acting.

By sheer chance, Emma's down-to-earth background had trained her in one of the most important principles of MLM prospecting—be yourself. While many novice prospectors waste time memorizing sales scripts and boning up on technical points about the product, experienced network marketers have learned that the most effective sales pitch is to just tell your story.

It doesn't need to be an epic saga, filled with suspense and pathos. It can be something as simple as, "I started taking these vitamin supplements, and my sinus headaches cleared right up," or "I worked night and day, seven days a week, and after a few months, I was making enough money to quit my job and go full-time in the business."

The important thing is that your story be true, and that it come from the heart. If you believe in your product and your opportunity, if you can relate your experience in simple conversational terms, then you are already armed with one of the most potent weapons in the Wave-Three prospector's arsenal.

Emma's Story

Emma's story, like most people's, was a simple one. After raising six children, she got divorced from her abusive husband and at the age of 57 went to work for the first time in her life, as a receptionist in an office building.

Emma hated working nine-to-five. But she saw no way out of it.

When she first tried network marketing, Emma's only hope was to earn a few hundred extra dollars per month, so she could finally afford to visit her out-of-state children. But Emma achieved far more than that. Through sheer hard work, she built a new life for herself. Today, as a full-time distributor for FreeLife, Emma earns more than $8,000 per month. The woman who had never traveled out of Missouri now vacations with her new husband in places like Europe, Hawaii, and the Caribbean. High-powered business leaders listen, rapt, to Emma's story when she addresses business briefings in cities like St. Louis and Omaha.

"My story is that I'm a very ordinary person," says Emma, "a mother and grandmother living in the heart of America, and if I can do it, you can do it too. It doesn't take some big hotshot person with a lot of professional experience. All you have to do is be yourself and tell your story."

A Level Playing Field

These were the thoughts that were going through Emma's head as she listened to the man on the telephone with ever-increasing irritation.

"Now, surely," he taunted her, "with all your success and all your, ahem, extensive experience in network marketing, you must have developed a philosophy of how to build this business. Why don't you just tell me your philosophy?"

In the long silence that followed, Emma could almost feel the man grinning on the other end of the line, waiting for her answer, so he could move in for the kill. In that instant, Emma realized that she had had just about enough of his condescension. He might be a big shot businessman from California and she a nobody from Missouri, but Emma didn't intend to be anyone's doormat.

Maybe she didn't have all the answers. Maybe she couldn't explain the business using all the technical jargon this man was accustomed to. But she knew how to make money in network marketing. And this character on the phone didn't have a clue about that.

Loosen Up

"All of a sudden, I just didn't care whether he joined up or not," says Emma. "And I didn't care what I said to him anymore. I don't use ugly language. I wasn't going to say anything like that. But, all of a sudden, I knew just what to say to him. It just popped into my head. And I thought, if he doesn't like it, that's just too bad."

Throughout the whole conversation, Emma had felt backed into a corner. She had been trying to speak a language that was alien to her, trying to live up to someone else's expectations. But Emma knew what it really took to work this business, and it had nothing to do with all that fancy businessman's talk. Emma decided to lay it on the line.

"Sure, I've got a philosophy for you," Emma said, with a hint of mischief in her voice. "Are you ready to hear it?"

"I'm ready," he said. "I've got my pen out. Tell it to me."

"Well, here it is," said Emma, deliberately sliding into her slowest, molasses-thick Missouri drawl. "My philosophy is: Late to bed, early to rise, work like crazy, and *advertise.*"

There was a long pause on the other end of the line. Then Emma could hear her prospect laughing. But he wasn't laughing at her. He was laughing at himself.

"I hear you," he finally said. "That's your philosophy and it's working. I guess that's good enough."

"He just loosened right up after that," says Emma. "He signed up and placed an order on the spot."

The Narrative Instinct

"I often avoid a long and useless discussion . . . or a laborious explanation . . ." said Abraham Lincoln, ". . . by a short story that illustrates my point of view." (Donald Phillips, *Lincoln on Leadership,* Warner Books, New York, 1992). Lincoln was one of the great storytellers of all time. He understood that to tell people stories was a faster, surer, and easier route to their hearts than any "useless discussion" or "laborious explanation." Successful network marketers have learned the same lesson.

The knack for storytelling is engraved in our brains as deeply as our instinct for eating and sleeping. Anyone can do it. If you fuss and fret over what to say to your prospects, you'll probably only bore them. But if you relax, take a deep breath, and just *tell your story,* then, like gasoline at the flare of a match, your downline will respond with hair-trigger sensitivity.

THE STORY-BUILDING STRATEGY

When people ask Colli Butler what she does for a living, she tells them, "I'm a professional storyteller. I tell stories for a living. My first one's free. Would you like to hear it?"

If the answer is yes, Colli then treats her prospects to one of the most powerful network marketing stories ever told—her own. As the leading distributors for FreeLife International, Colli and her husband, David, tell a tale with a very happy ending. But their story wasn't always so rosy. Colli and David went through tough times. Between the two of them, they worked with nine different MLM companies, six of which went out of business. The Butlers lost their home, their savings, and, at one point, built up half a million dollars in debt.

As they battled their way up from the bottom, the last thing Colli and David wanted was to let their prospects know how badly they were struggling. They were too embarrassed to simply tell their story as it was. The Butlers were forced to learn the fine art of *story-building*—constructing and using effective success stories, even during periods when your personal saga is less than inspiring.

Today, Colli and David have nothing more to hide. Through story-building, they have rescued themselves from financial disaster. In the process, they have transformed their lives into an inspiring—and duplicatable—tale of courage, persistence, and redemption.

A Need for Cash

Colli Butler was used to doing without. Her parents could not afford to send her to college, so Colli worked as a telephone installer and, later, as a police dispatcher. She married young and ended up divorced, with an 11-month-old baby and a second child on the way.

As a single mother, Colli learned early the value of a healthy cash flow. She needed a lot of income to support herself and her children. So Colli set high goals. As a police dispatcher, she had to be available to work any shift, night or day. In addition, she sold real estate and obtained a license to sell insurance.

"I did anything I could on the side to make additional income," says Colli, "because I wanted a lot more out of life than I was getting."

A Man with a Past

Little wonder that Colli fell for an entrepreneur. David Butler had never pulled a paycheck in his entire life. He had always been his own boss. When she met and married David, Colli thought her struggles were over. After all, David owned a successful business and seemed to be headed places. What Colli didn't realize, however, is that, after seven years of self-employment, David was fast reaching the end of his rope.

"He was working hard and had no residual income," says Colli. "David was miserable."

Like all business owners, David had surrendered his freedom. And he was beginning to feel the loss. Employees pilfered his store. The government kept changing the licensing regulations. Once he got a call at 3 A.M. because someone had broken into his business. Another time, an employee called in sick just as he and Colli were on their way to church. David had to drop everything and run to the store.

Colli and David sold the business and tried selling insurance for a while. But they didn't like that business either. One day, David came to Colli and made a confession. He revealed to her a whole past life that he'd never told her about—his life as a network marketer.

"Colli, I want to tell you about the most fun I've ever had, and the most money I have ever made in my life," David began. "It was with network marketing. *And I want to get back into it.*"

The Bug

Colli was not only shocked, she was appalled. *Why can't he just get a job like other men?* she thought. But aloud, Colli smiled and tried to be supportive.

The tale David told was hardly encouraging. He had managed to work his way up to $50,000 per month with one MLM company. But then it went out of business. The next two companies he tried also failed. It was then that David had quit the industry in disgust and vowed never to come back. He had kept his promise for seven years.

But once you've got the bug, David explained, you can never completely shake it. It's like a little voice inside saying, *Give it one more chance.* David knew in his heart that MLM held the secret of financial freedom for him and his family, if he could only find the right opportunity. Colli gave her grudging assent.

Build a Story Line

David then got involved with a company selling fiber-rich weight-loss cookies. Although Colli made it clear she wanted nothing to do with the business, she soon found that she liked the cookies and began taking them to work.

Colli's job as a police dispatcher gave no meal breaks, so she had to wolf down her food right at her radio console during the few seconds she got between phone calls and radio transmissions. The cookies made a perfect meal replacement. Soon, other employees followed Colli's example and started eating the cookies in lieu of lunch. Many claimed they lost weight in the process.

"Then, on pay day," says Colli, "people would get their checks and complain about how little they were making. So I told them about my husband's business and how they could make a few hundred dollars a month part-time."

Although she never intended to, Colli had built her first MLM *story line*—a compact narrative that inspires interest in your business.

A story line can cover anything from your company and its products to your personal achievements and dreams for the future. You need no professional skills to tell a story. The only requirement is that your story be true. People will shy away from a phony story, no matter how glib your presentation. But if you speak from the heart, you will draw prospects like a magnet.

In Colli's mind, the cookie company had always been "David's business," not hers. She was just making small talk with her friends. But Colli's story line intrigued people. One by one, they started signing up.

Unexpected Fruit

A few months after starting the business, David was examining his monthly printout from the company. This is a computer-generated list showing every distributor in David's downline. On this particular month, David noticed something strange. He was unable to recognize many of the names on the list. David asked his wife who they were.

"It turned out they were all people I had signed up," says Colli. "David told me I had recruited more people into the business that month than he had!"

What amazed Colli is that she hadn't even been trying. For the first time, she began to grasp the power of network marketing—a business you could build just by *telling stories*. At last, Colli began taking an active role. It wasn't long before her monthly income was in the five figures.

The Hard Facts of MLM

Experts estimate that over 90 percent of MLM companies fail within their first 18 months. David had already learned this hard fact of life, through years of disappointment and setbacks. Now it was Colli's turn. No sooner had she begun to build an impressive downline than the cookie company suddenly went out of business.

"I was devastated," says Colli. "But now I had caught the bug too. All I wanted was to find the next opportunity and start rebuilding."

Running the Show

David and Colli then tried to start their own MLM business. For the first year and a half, things went well. The new company sold a line of breakfast cereals, granola bars, nutritional supplements, and a colloidal mineral drink. Company-wide sales grew, at one point, to $200,000 per month. But David and Colli had yet to make a profit.

"I still worked full-time as a police dispatcher on the graveyard shift," said Colli, "and then worked on our company during the day."

David and Colli set up a corporate office with a bed in the back room. When she got off her shift, Colli would collapse on the bed, then rise a few hours later to open the office and work until late in the evening. The only nights she slept at home were on weekends and on her days off from the police dispatcher job. David worked virtually nonstop, seven days a week.

Half a Million in Debt

Disaster struck swiftly. Colli and David were lured into partnership with an MLM hype artist who offered exclusive new product lines and access to international markets. Four months later, their company was out of business.

According to Colli, the new partners flew "hotshot" network marketers in from all over the country, put them up in fancy hotels, and wined and dined them—all on the Butlers' credit cards. They hired employees who didn't work out. They poured tens of thousands of dollars into producing inferior sales literature that had to be thrown out.

"The bills added up quickly," says Colli, "and we did not have that kind of capital. The next thing I knew, we were half a million dollars in debt, and our partners vanished, leaving us holding the bag."

Ruined!

Colli and David were ruined. With no income except what Colli made at her job, they somehow had to pay $10,000 in bills every month. Bankruptcy seemed the only option. The Butlers hired an attorney and completed all the paperwork.

"But something inside kept us from filing," says Colli. "I kept thinking, if we really believe in network marketing and the opportunity it provides for us, then we have to keep going. I was sure we could pay this debt off!"

Selective Story-Building

Now David and Colli faced a challenge. In a business that works by storytelling, they would somehow have to succeed without telling their story! After all, how many prospects could you entice by saying, "We failed at five different MLM companies and now we're half a million dollars in debt!"

To supplement their income while they searched for a new opportunity, David began offering generic MLM seminars. There, he would teach the nuts and bolts of building a downline, without recommending any particular company. When he took the podium, David shared story after story about his past successes. But he kept quiet about his current financial struggles. For years, the Butlers labored quietly to pay off their debt, somehow managing to keep any word of their current predicament from leaking out to industry gossips.

False Stories

In the meantime, David and Colli continued their quest for the perfect MLM company. There were times when it seemed hopeless. Every opportunity they tried turned out to have some hidden flaw. In the end, David and Colli would always find themselves sitting in front of some prospect, trying to tell a story that, deep down in their hearts, they really didn't believe.

"We made really good money in one company," Colli recalls. "But within a year, we discovered that most of the people we had brought into the business were not earning money. The amount of group volume required to get your check each month was so high, most of our distributors were not able to achieve it. We felt like we were setting people up for failure."

A Desperate Move

For the Butlers, even darker days lay ahead. After suffering her third miscarriage in a row, Colli was forced to take a medical leave of absence from her job. Now MLM provided their only income.

"Creditors were calling day and night," says Colli. "We used our MasterCard to pay Visa and our Visa to pay personal loans."

The Butlers made a tough decision. David was offered a job consulting for a network marketing company in Newport Beach, California. That meant he would get a salary, in addition to having the opportunity to build a downline. Colli was now pregnant with their sixth child. After much discussion and prayer, they decided that Colli would stay home while David would move to Newport Beach to work the business.

"David and I have always been very close and would not normally have considered living apart," says Colli. "But we decided he would be more productive in California."

When It Rains, It Pours

For all practical purposes, Colli was back to being a single mother. Nine months pregnant and sharing a tiny, three-bedroom house with three children (the oldest children had already moved out), there were times when it was all Colli could do to maintain her sanity. And things just kept getting worse.

One day, a storm tore the roof off their house. The ceiling collapsed in several places. Water was an inch deep on every floor and the carpet was ruined. Tens of thousands of dollars worth of fax machines, computers, and other office equipment were destroyed by water. But the insurance company refused to pay for either the machines or the roof.

"My children and I wore snow boots in the house to keep from getting our feet wet," says Colli.

Right at that time, Colli had to run a meeting at a local hotel to introduce new prospects to her MLM business. It wasn't until she arrived that Colli realized she'd forgotten to put on her high heels.

"I walked into the hotel dressed in a nice business dress, nylons and . . . oh my gosh, no! PINK SNOW BOOTS! I knew right then life could not get any worse."

But Colli was wrong. They could still get a lot worse. And they did.

Back to Square One

At night, when Colli found herself weeping alone in the dark, she would often console herself with the thought that her sacrifice at least freed David to work hard and build for their future. Down in Newport Beach, David worked like a madman. He put in 16-hour days, sleeping at the office and returning to his apartment only to shower and change. Each month, his check got a little bigger, his downline deeper and wider.

But then, almost like the punch line to some bizarre cosmic joke, the company *went out of business!* When she heard the news, Colli thought she must be hallucinating. But it was all too real. For the seventh time in a row, network marketing had let them down. They had suffered and sacrificed for nothing.

Pay the Price

In no other industry is persistence rewarded as surely and bountifully as in network marketing. But in no other industry is it demanded to such an extreme. MLM exacts a dreadful toll from each and every one of its successful practitioners. Yet, even amid such prodigies of faith and endurance, the tenacity of David and Colli Butler stands out as something special.

"Most people give up just when they're about to achieve success," said H. Ross Perot. "They quit on the one yard line. They give up at the last minute of the game, one foot from a winning touchdown."

Whether they knew it or not, the Butlers were right on the brink of a winning touchdown. But it would take every remaining ounce of their faith to crawl that final yard into the end zone.

MINGLED DESTINIES

Right about the time that David and Colli Butler were trying to get their ill-fated breakfast-cereal company off the ground, a Yale law student named Ray Faltinsky was reading a column in the May 1990 issue of *Success* magazine. Neither Ray nor the Butlers knew of each others' existence. But they were destined to play an extraordinary role in each others' lives.

The column Ray was reading was entitled "Network Marketing: The Most Powerful Way to Reach Consumers in the 1990s."

"It was my first exposure to network marketing," Ray recalls. "I fell in love with the concept immediately."

Ray's parents had come over from Europe in 1955 unable to speak English and with little more than the clothes on their backs. With four children to support, his father held down three jobs while his mother worked part-time at a local bakery and a five-and-dime store.

"It always seemed weird to me, as a kid," says Ray, "that no matter how hard my parents worked, we never really had any financial security. Even just a few years ago, my parents had to move because they couldn't afford the real estate taxes anymore."

Man with a Mission

Ray Faltinsky entered law school with a mission.

"My overriding goal," he says, "was to research what avenues existed for the average person to achieve financial security, even without a college degree."

Two of Ray's professors recommended that he investigate franchising. But Ray found that franchises can cost from $80,000 to a million dollars or more. People like his parents could never afford that kind of money.

Then Ray stumbled upon the article in *Success*. Here was a business you could work from home, for a small investment, and on a part-time basis, if you wished—and still have the potential for unlimited income. The more Ray studied the industry, the more excited he became. For a while, he even became a distributor himself for an MLM company selling nutritional products.

"I found that you could join most companies for $50 to $100," says Ray. "And you didn't need any special skills or education to get involved. I was absolutely blown away by the industry. I spent the next two years researching everything I could about it."

In fact, Ray ended up writing his law school thesis on the network marketing industry. When he first pitched the idea to some business law professors at Yale, they laughed. But, in the end, Ray obtained special permission from Guido Calabresi, the dean of Yale Law School, who offered to personally supervise the paper. Calabresi even provided funding for Ray to travel the country, interviewing some of the top experts and achievers in MLM.

"I saw that this whole industry was going to explode over the next five to ten years for two reasons," says Ray. "First, because of the downsizing in corporate America, and second, because network marketing provided something the business world needed—word-of-mouth advertising, which is, without a doubt, the most effective form of advertising in existence."

The Hand of Fate

As if through some strange alchemy of fate, *Success* magazine continued to drive the destiny of this energetic and impassioned young man. One day in 1992, Ray was poring over an issue of the magazine while working out on an exercycle. His attention was caught by a brief story about a professor at the University of Alberta who claimed to have invented a candy bar that actually *burned* fat. The more candy bars you ate, the less you weighed.

"What a great product to spread through word of mouth," thought Ray. "It's perfect for network marketing."

Ray had just received his copy of *Success* in the mail. He knew that subscribers got the magazine before it hit the newsstand. That meant Ray had a head start. Leaping from his bike, Ray sprinted from the gym to his New Haven apartment and called the University of Alberta. Within minutes, he was talking to Professor Larry Wang.

"I have a great idea for this product," Ray told him. "I want to meet with you."

Ray was on the next flight to Alberta and met with Professor Wang the following day. In a short time, Ray had brokered a deal between the professor and a network marketing company called Melaleuca in Idaho Falls, Idaho. Melaleuca distributes the product today.

"That bar has become one of the biggest selling nutrition products ever," says Ray. "It has sold millions of units in two years, and I get a royalty every time someone buys a bar."

A Company Is Born

But that success only whetted Ray's appetite for more. What he really wanted was an MLM company of his own. Ray knew that network marketing in the '90s required sophisticated computer systems and top-rate sales tools. That meant big money. Where would he get it?

One day, Ray was having lunch with a law school friend and talking about his idea for a company called FreeLife.

"You might want to talk to my godfather," said the friend. "He just retired from an investment banking firm in New York and he'd like to invest in a startup company. He's a multimillionaire."

Within a few weeks, Ray had met with the godfather and secured his seed capital. Anyone who has ever tried to raise money will realize how unlikely it is to run into a wealthy godfather at just the moment you need him. But, in the mysteriously charmed life of Ray Faltinsky, such serendipities had become almost routine. Other investors soon followed, including Ray's current partner, Kevin Fournier. It wasn't long before Ray was ready to go to work.

Ray had become a nutrition enthusiast. In the 1980s, his mother was cured of the crippling case of osteoporosis through the use of nutritional supplements. Then his

sister-in-law's breast cancer disappeared—without sur-
gery—after she used supplements. Impressed by these results, Ray made it his mission to bring this lifesaving
information to the world. He determined that network
marketing would provide the perfect vehicle.

Ray knew that the aging of the 76 million baby
boomers ensured that the nutrition industry would triple
over the next 10 years, to $100 billion or more. But to
reach that market, FreeLife would have to offer something new and unique. In quest of a product line, Ray met
with top research scientists at Yale and traveled the country talking to experts. But he couldn't find any product
with the right pizzazz.

Then, one day in 1993, Ray struck up a conversation
with the woman sitting next to him in a Los Angeles hair
salon. It turned out she was the agent and business manager for Dr. Earl Mindell, generally recognized as the
world's leading authority on nutrition. Mindell's *Vitamin
Bible* alone had sold over 7.5 million copies.

"Well, gee," said Ray. "What's Dr. Mindell up to these
days? Working on anything exciting?"

As fate would have it, Mindell had just developed a
nutritional product line and was looking for a company to
market it. Nine months and six visits to Los Angeles
later, Mindell signed an exclusive contract with FreeLife
until the year 2010.

"Now we were ready to rock and roll," says Ray.

The Package

One day, not long after these events, Colli Butler received a
package in the mail from a man named Keith McEachern
of New Fairfield, Connecticut.

She didn't have to open it to know what it was. Colli
and David received about ten such MLM pitches per day.
As well-known "heavy hitters," they seemed to be on

every mailing list in the industry. Usually, Colli glanced at them for a second, threw them on David's pile, and never gave them a second thought. But this time, Colli hesitated. She recognized the name Keith McEachern. He was a major distributor for a leading MLM company. Colli had spoken to him once on the phone after responding to one of his ads in *USA Today.* Colli opened the package with interest. Out fell an audiocassette tape, a letter, and a paperback book. The book was called *Earl Mindell's Soy Miracle.*

The Mindell Gimmick

Nutrition, Colli thought, with a smile. *He must be pitching a nutrition company.* The book by Mindell was a dead giveaway. Colli had often used the Mindell gimmick herself. Any time you were selling a nutritional product, you could almost always find some angle to bring in Earl Mindell—the world's leading nutritionist—as a "third-party validation." If you were selling an herbal product, you might quote some supportive phrase from Mindell's *Herb Bible.* If it was a vitamin product, you could refer your prospects to Mindell's *Vitamin Bible.* And so on.

You could hardly find a better "third party." In addition to the best-selling *Vitamin Bible,* Mindell was constantly appearing on TV talk shows. You literally couldn't walk into a nutrition store without seeing Mindell's face smiling from the covers of a dozen paperbacks on the book rack. When you dealt with nutritional products and nutrition-oriented people, Mindell's name was magic.

Colli figured that Keith McEachern must be pushing some kind of soy product. So including *Earl Mindell's Soy Miracle* was a smart move. *Go for it, Keith,* Colli grinned.

Then she started reading the letter. From that moment on, Colli Butler's life would never be the same.

The Ultimate Story

It was only a few seconds later that Colli went rushing into David's office, her heart pounding in excitement.

"David!" she cried. "You've got to look at this. You just won't believe it."

David peered up at her. He was on the phone. Ordinarily, Colli never interrupted him at such times. But now she insisted that David get off the phone and listen to her.

"David, there's a new network marketing company that just launched with products developed by Dr. Earl Mindell," Colli announced. "He has an exclusive contract with them. I bet this is going to be hot!"

David nodded vaguely and took the letter. "I'll take a look at it," he said distractedly. "Okay?"

Colli left David's office with a horrible feeling of disappointment. *He's not interested!* she thought. *He's just going to sit there and let this opportunity pass us by.* It took the rest of the day for Colli to calm down. She prided herself on not being a nag. So, for the next two weeks, Colli tried her best not to think about the magical package sitting unread on David's "in" pile.

The Naked Truth

Then, one day, David came racing out of his office in excitement.

"Colli!" he cried. "You're not going to believe this. There's a new MLM company with an exclusive deal on Dr. Earl Mindell's products!"

It turned out that David had only been half listening before. When he finally got around to reading Keith McEachern's cover letter, David recognized the titles of Mindell's books, and the whole concept finally clicked. Then the two of them sat down and listened to the audiotape Keith McEachern had sent.

"When I first heard about FreeLife," said Keith, "I was already the top distributor with a truly great network marketing company, and I did not plan to make a change. But when I heard this story, it was magic. I knew I had to be a part of it."

Keith went on to say that Ray Faltinsky was a close personal friend, and that they had first met at Yale. "Ray is a golden boy," said Keith, with utter conviction in his voice. "Everything he touches turns to gold. He's one of those people who is destined for success."

David and Colli listened with a kind of quiet awe. There was power in Keith's words, the power of total honesty. He wasn't pushing anything on them, because he didn't have to. It was one of those rare moments in network marketing, when the sheer, naked truth was all you needed.

No Compromise

Before they met each other, Colli and David had both spent many years searching for a mate. Both were divorced. Both had had many chances to remarry. But they had turned them all down, breaking off one relationship after another if it didn't seem right. Friends and relatives had warned them not to be so choosy.

"Your standards are too high," they would say. "If you don't learn to compromise, you'll end up being lonely all your life."

But David and Colli didn't listen to their advice. They just kept searching until, at last, they found one another. "Once we met," says Colli, "we knew absolutely that 'this is the person I can spend the rest of my life with.'"

Because they had succeeded, against all odds, in finding their perfect love, Colli and David knew instinctively that they could also find their ultimate opportunity. You didn't have to compromise. If you kept on looking, and refused to settle for second best, you would eventually find your perfect company.

"After so many disappointments," says Colli, "we had reached the point where we almost didn't believe any longer that the perfect company existed, the one that when you join, you develop a passion and belief so strong that you sacrifice everything to build it."

But, as they sat together that day, listening to Keith McEachern's tape, David and Colli felt an emotion pass between them that they had almost despaired of ever feeling—a deep, glowing certainty in their hearts that *this was the one.* Their long, painful search had finally come to an end.

Total Commitment

It had been a long time since David and Colli had geared up for a push like this. But they hadn't lost the edge. They could feel the excitement rising like sap in their limbs. And this time, they were determined to make it work.

"We had a meeting with our children," Colli says, "and we all agreed we would sacrifice everything for one year. No PTA for me. No going on field trips with my children. No extracurricular church activities. No family vacations, except at Christmas."

Then David and Colli went for it. Six days a week, they worked 12- to 16-hour days, resting only on Sundays ("to thank the Lord," says Colli). At first, they rented an office. But they found that they lost too much time driving back and forth, so they started working from home.

"We lived the business," says Colli. "From the time I woke up in the morning to the time I went to bed at night, which was often three or four o'clock in the morning, this was all I did."

The X Factor

Colli's pitch was simple. She just gave them the naked truth. And she didn't waste any words dressing it up. "Have you ever heard of Dr. Earl Mindell?" she would ask.

In most cases, the answer was yes. But if prospects said no, she would press, "Well, have you ever heard of the *Vitamin Bible?*" For those prospects with no background in nutrition at all, Colli would issue this challenge: "Let me give you this audiocassette tape. Go home, look in your phone book, call a couple of nutrition stores, call your local library, call Barnes and Noble, and just ask them about Dr. Earl Mindell and his books. Then listen to the tapes. I'll call you tomorrow."

Most prospects didn't need much more persuasion than that. Colli called it the "X Factor"—the massive power of Dr. Earl Mindell's reputation.

"It's a story that's very easy to tell," she says.

Redemption

As expected, FreeLife quickly became one of the fastest-growing companies in network marketing. After a year in business, its downline was growing at 25 percent to 40 percent per month. As this book goes to press, about 35 percent of those distributors are in David and Colli Butler's downline, and the couple's latest monthly check was for $60,000.

The Butlers recently paid off the last penny of their half-million dollar debt. They also bought a 6,000-square-foot home (with its own dock and beach) on a private lake in a prestigious, gated, Southern California community.

No longer do the Butlers need to hide behind other people's stories. Now they can proudly tell their own, explaining to prospects how FreeLife and the "X Factor" rescued them from unspeakable debt and freed them from financial worries.

The Dream

The Butlers have lived an incredible saga of pain, courage, and redemption. When they tell their story, they need no hype, no embellishments. The naked truth speaks for itself.

At long last, the Butlers have reached the point where they have begun throttling back. A year and a half after starting their FreeLife business, they worked only half days through the whole summer, and, in the fall, cut back their workday to a normal 40-hour week.

"We worked hard to get where we are and have earned the right to enjoy our lifestyle," says Colli. "Three to five years from now we will work one to two hours per day and show up at major company events, and that will be the extent of it. That's what the Dream is all about."

For the Butlers, the Dream has become a reality. A fairy tale woven in their minds many years ago has become the true story of their lives. The longer they suffered and struggled, the better their story grew, until today, duplicated on audiocassettes and disseminated by the thousands to their downline, the Butlers' years of suffering and hardship have at last been transmuted into an unstoppable juggernaut of persuasive power, a story that few prospects can resist.

"I think the Lord tests people sometimes," says David Butler. "I think Colli and I had to go through these trials to prove that we were worthy of success. No matter how bad things got, we never lost faith. We never stopped believing in this industry. I always knew that if we kept looking, we'd find the right story to tell."

Chapter 6

CATCH A BIG FISH

C ell Tech may be one of the least likely success stories in network marketing. For nearly ten years, its single product was dried algae, dispensed in capsules. Its only customers, for many years, were a tiny subculture of hard-core health food enthusiasts. Yet, Cell Tech has broken dramatically into the mainstream, becoming one of the fastest-growing MLM companies of the 1990s. Between 1991 and 1996, the number of Cell Tech distributors increased over ten times, from about 30,000 to over 350,000.

In large measure, Cell Tech owes its success to a single man, named Showshawme. Over *90 percent* of the company's distributors are in his downline. Showshawme is a "big fish." He's the sort of catch for which every new distributor in network marketing is avidly angling. Yet, Showshawme is no superman. He has no special skills or unusual techniques. How did he do it? Simple. Showshawme recruited *other* big fish.

"My income didn't come from sponsoring lots of people," he says. "It came from sponsoring only two or three mainlines. And from those two or three people, hundreds of thousands of other people have come."

It's Not Luck—It's Strategy

The uninformed would say that Showshawme "just got lucky." Indeed, it remains a widespread myth in network marketing that the only way to catch big fish is to spread your net wide and keep your fingers crossed. But that's not how it works. Luck will seldom lead you to the right people. Nor will it tell you how to reel them in, once they've nipped at the bait. Like prize trout in a stream, big fish in MLM can only be landed through strategy and planning.

Showshawme targeted his fish with a shrewd eye to their personal and professional spheres of influence. Before he recruited them, he knew exactly who he wanted and precisely how they would help his business. Then Showshawme zeroed in on his prospects with relentless persistence and won them to his cause.

In Chapter 3, readers were advised to turn down the pressure in prospecting. This is good advice, in most cases. But when the stakes are high and the prospects are as valuable as those Showshawme had in his sights, it is sometimes wise to suspend the rules. One or two big fish can make the difference between success and mediocrity in your network marketing business. Knowing whom to target and when to turn on the pressure are key skills that, when mastered, have the potential to turbocharge your downline with an extraordinary Butterfly Effect.

High School Dropout

Showshawme's parents were hardworking, middle-class people in the Hartford, Connecticut, suburbs. Unfortunately, both parents were heavy drinkers and often beat Showshawme for little or no reason. He grew into a nervous, angry little boy, getting in frequent fights and doing poorly in school. By the age of 14, he was drinking, sniffing glue, and dabbling with drugs.

"I dropped out of high school in tenth grade," says Showshawme. "I almost committed suicide through drug abuse."

Showshawme was 18 years old when he checked into a drug rehabilitation program. By that time, he'd been arrested twice on drug charges and had a school record that wouldn't land him a job as dog catcher. But Showshawme was alive. His six months in rehab proved a turning point. There, he received his high school diploma and set out on the long, slow road to redemption.

New Age Zealots

"I didn't have any meaning or purpose in my life," says Showshawme. "I was searching for something."

In his quest for enlightenment, Showshawme wandered far off the beaten path. He turned to books like *Wisdom of the Mystic Masters,* which imparted the esoteric teachings of the Rosicrucians. He acquired a Hindu guru and swore off meat. Like so many others in the early '70s, Showshawme was drawn into the "alternative" subculture—that growing network of ex-hippies, tree-huggers, herb lovers, and spiritual seekers whose co-op groceries, esoteric bookstores, vegetarian cafes, and shiatsu clinics were even then springing up like mushrooms in countercultural enclaves across the country.

The "alternative" crowd steadfastly maintained that America's lust for profits was destroying the environment. They taught that money corrupted the soul. Yet, ironically, it was through this very network of New Age zealots that Showshawme would one day build his incredible fortune.

A Flair for Business

Showshawme had cleansed himself of drugs. But he remained a tormented man. For a while, he worked in a factory. For nine and a half hours a day, at two dollars an hour, Showshawme drilled holes in three-inch socket extensions, one after another.

"It was a terrible robot-type job," says Showshawme. "I'd look at the owner of the company and think, 'This guy has money and we're just a bunch of peons working and hating it.' I wanted to get out, but I didn't know how."

Deep in his heart, Showshawme wanted money. Lots of it. But his spiritual beliefs required him to renounce such "material" ambitions. That wasn't easy for Showshawme. From an early age, he had shown an aptitude for business.

"As a paper boy, when I was 12 or 13, I won all the contests for getting the most customers," says Showshawme. "I was very enterprising."

Compromise

For years, Showshawme sought a compromise between his business ambitions and his New Age beliefs. He tried selling "alternative" products, such as alfalfa sprouts grown in buckets in his bathtub, bee pollen supplements, or pyramid-power knickknacks. But Showshawme's deep-rooted fear of money kept him from succeeding.

"Because of my parents' alcoholism," says Showshawme, "I associated money with misery. No matter how many material goods they had—a bigger house, a newer car—they were still miserable. So I felt that money was evil. It didn't make you happy."

New Name, New Life

By the time he was 28 years old, Showshawme's internal conflicts had reached an unbearable intensity. It was time for radical action. In order to make a complete break with his past, he changed his name legally to "Showshawme."

Then, with only a one-way ticket and $200 in his pocket, Showshawme pulled up stakes and moved to Hawaii. "I wanted to eat a healthier diet and breathe healthier air," Showshawme explains. "I was searching for my soul, trying to figure out what I wanted to do with my life."

Down and out in Hawaii

At first, Showshawme stayed with friends. Then he moved into the jungle and lived in a tent. Showshawme rationalized his primitive existence as a spiritual journey. He told himself that he was renouncing the corruption of Western civilization. But when the rains poured and the tent stank of mildew, when rats chewed through the tent fabric to get at his food and mosquitoes swarmed night and day, there were times when Showshawme couldn't help having second thoughts.

"I had pictured Hawaii as sunshine, clear skies, sandy beaches," he says. "But where I lived, on the east side of the big island of Hawaii, it was real rough. It rained all the time, there were no sandy beaches, and there was an active volcano. A lot of people were living in the woods without plumbing or electricity. There was a lot of poverty."

No More Safety Net

For two years, Showshawme lived in that tent, catching rainwater to drink and buying his groceries with food stamps. He also sold natural foods to the local food co-op. Showshawme would wholesale dried seaweed and sell alfalfa sprouts that he grew in a friend's garage. But, despite all his efforts, he still couldn't make ends meet.

As long as his parents lived, Showshawme had a financial safety net. They would send him money when things got tight. But, one day, Showshawme got word that his mother had suddenly died. His father went soon after, from an apparent stroke. The shock of this double loss was more than emotional for Showshawme. It hit him right in his pocketbook.

"All of a sudden," says Showshawme, "I couldn't call home anymore to get help. There was nobody there. I was all alone. That's when I realized I had to become self-reliant. I had to do something."

But Showshawme had no idea what that something might be. The local economy was poor. Jobs were scarce. Confused and depressed, Showshawme searched for a way out of his plight. Little did he realize that escape was right around the corner.

An Unexpected Solution

The answer to Showshawme's problem actually began to take form about 7,000 years before. That's when an immense volcano near what is now the west coast of the United States blew its top, spewing five cubic miles of earth into the air. The blast was so powerful that huge boulders rained down as far away as present-day Idaho.

Near the volcano, millions of tons of mineral ash blanketed the earth. Rainwater washed those minerals into rivers and streams, carrying them down into the basin of a great mountain lake in what is now the state of Oregon. For 7,000 years, the process continued, until the lake—now called Upper Klamath Lake—was filled with up to 35 feet of nutrient-rich sediment, providing a fertile growth environment for a unique type of algae.

Algae: The Oldest Food on Earth

Algae is among the world's most ancient and most successful organisms, possibly as much as three and a half

billion years old. When bacteria—the first life-form on
earth—learned to turn sunlight into energy through pho-
tosynthesis, they became "blue-green algae"—a family
whose progeny still thrive to this day.

There are some 30,000 algae species, which can take
any form from microscopic "pond scum" to giant marine
colonies called sea kelps hundreds of feet long. Representing 70 percent of the earth's biomass, it is algae—not rain
forests—that provides 80 percent of the planet's oxygen.

From Central America to Africa, from the "seaweed"
familiar to sushi lovers to the *Spirulina* once harvested
by the Aztecs from Lake Texcoco, algae—in its red, green,
brown, golden, and blue-green varieties—has long been a
source of essential vitamins, minerals, and protein for
millions of human beings. Closer to home, health food enthusiasts have promoted algae-eating since the 1970s,
claiming unusual nutritive effects from improved mental
clarity to tumor reduction.

A Starving World

According to some environmentalists, for the last 10,000
years, erosion, farming, and, more recently, the use of
chemical fertilizers have all been slowly leeching the fer-
tility from North American topsoil.

As a result of this soil depletion, some experts believe
that vegetables no longer contain the high level of nutri-
ents they once did. Some researchers have reported that
100 grams of spinach had only one-seventieth the amount
of iron in 1973 that it did in 1948, according to Linda
Grover in her book *August Celebration: A Molecule of Hope
for Changing the World* (Gilbert, Hoover & Clark, 1993).
Other authorities say that the amount of beta-carotene in
3.5 ounces of raw carrots can vary today from 18,000 IU
(International Units) to only 70, as reported by Dr.
Michael Colgan in *Your Personal Vitamin Profile*. Eating

such depleted vegetables may leave your belly full but
your body starved for nutrition.

The Algae Solution

Some researchers suggest that algae might provide an alternative to today's bleached-out vegetables. Unfortunately, most of the lakes, ponds, and coastlines where wild
algae grows are now polluted. Attempts to grow it artifi-
cially have met with mixed success. But in the early
1980s, scientist, educator, and entrepreneur Daryl J. Kollman discovered a particularly nutritious strain of blue-
green algae—*Aphanizomenon flos aquae*—growing wild in
Oregon's Upper Klamath Lake. It was a common species,
but it was transformed by the lake's unique ecology into a
new, supernutritious strain, which Kollman named Super
Blue Green Algae.

Isolated high in the remote Cascade Mountains, the
lake remains pure and clean to this day. Kollman claims
that each inch of its rich, volcanic sediment is sufficient to
keep the lake's blue-green algae packed with nutrition for
60 years. With 200 million pounds of Super Blue Green
Algae growing in the lake every year, the algae replen-
ishes itself as fast as it is harvested. Kollman calculates
that the lake could potentially produce enough algae for
every person on earth to eat 1 to 2 grams per day.

"It's simply the most powerful food, the most powerful source of nutrition on the planet," says Kollman.
"There is nothing else like it. You can't get that energy
anymore from broccoli, cauliflower, and beans."

Energy and Clarity

When Showshawme first heard the Super Blue Green
Algae story from a friend at the local food co-op, he was
skeptical. But then he tried it for himself.

"Within half an hour," Showshawme recalls, "I felt a tremendous surge of energy and crystal-clear clarity. I felt like doing somersaults over the tent."

Showshawme became an algae dealer. Cell Tech hadn't yet been founded, so Showshawme ordered the algae from a company in Arizona run by Daryl Kollman's brother. "I would buy it in bulk," says Showshawme, "and borrow scales from people who were growing marijuana on the island. I didn't do drugs myself anymore, but I used the scales to weigh up the algae and sell little bags to people, marking it up just enough to pay for one meal a day. It wasn't easy. I was just barely in survival mode for quite some time."

COMING AWAKE

True believers in the Cell Tech philosophy preach that the algae cleanses the body and stimulates the mind in subtle and mysterious ways. Showshawme is convinced that the algae awakened him from his long, spiritual doldrums and drove him to become more productive.

"I felt more alive than I ever had before," he says. "I couldn't keep to myself in the woods anymore. I felt I just had to do something. I had to get out and tell people about this incredible algae."

In the summer of 1985, Showshawme moved back to Connecticut. He was a very different man from the one who had left nearly five years before. Showshawme's years in the wilderness had chastened him and filled him with a mighty resolve. He was tired of living on the fringes of society. He was weary of spouting rhetoric about changing the world when he didn't even have the power to pay his own bills. Showshawme had learned at last that the first step to changing the world was to change yourself.

"I had been an ineffective radical," says Showshawme. "Now I wanted to become an effective radical."

A Money Magnet

At the root of Showshawme's ineffectiveness was his lingering guilt about making money. He knew it was holding him back. So he set out to change it. Showshawme began an intensive regimen of self-improvement. He attended workshops and seminars, listened to tapes, and read inspirational books such as *Think and Grow Rich* and *The Richest Man in Babylon.*

"I changed my belief systems," says Showshawme. "And when I did that, my life changed for the better."

Thousands of times per day, in the shower, in his car, in his apartment, Showshawme would repeat positive affirmations, such as, "I am now financially prosperous and successful." Acting on a suggestion he had read in a book, Showshawme even began carrying a $100 bill in his pocket at all times.

"When you do that, you can never say you're broke," he says. "And you draw prosperity to you like a money magnet."

A House Divided

Positive thinking and aggressive goal-setting soon made its mark on Showshawme's prospecting. His downline grew by the day. His phone rang off the hook with people who had heard about the algae and wanted to get involved.

Nevertheless, Showshawme's organization was growing too slowly for his taste. Having lived his entire adult life in the New Age subculture, Showshawme knew there were a lot more potential recruits out there than he was getting. Literally millions of people shared his views about natural food and healing. Why was he only able to recruit them a handful at a time?

Showshawme knew part of the answer already. He knew that the natural food community was a house divided. Each nutritional theory attracted its own acolytes, dedicated to a particular diet and often harshly critical of rivals. Selling the Cell Tech vision in that community was like preaching Christian Science to a roomful of Catholics and Southern Baptists.

Agents of Influence

But Showshawme had no choice. In 1985, mainstream America was not yet ready to buy capsules full of dried algae. Only the nutritional savants, already accustomed to herbal supplements, macrobiotic diets, and "live-food" regimens, would have the background to even comprehend his sales pitch, much less agree with it. Showshawme would have to penetrate these close-knit and potentially hostile communities. For that, he would need agents— people who were known and trusted in those communities, with access to wide circles of influence.

A FATEFUL PHONE CALL

To support himself, Showshawme worked a wide range of businesses, including selling macrobiotic supplies out of his tiny apartment in Hartford. After reading about an ancient South American grain called quinoa, Showshawme called up a local distributor to see about ordering some. It proved to be one of the most fateful calls of his life.

Showshawme ended up speaking to a woman named Kim Bright (who has now added the married name of Cassano). Not only did she own a natural food distribution company, but it turned out she was also a major force in the macrobiotic community. Kim ran a macrobiotic learning center and owned a macrobiotic restaurant called A Change of Seasons in Westport, Connecticut.

Showshawme immediately pitched her on the Super Blue Green Algae.

"That isn't a food," said Kim frostily. "That is a supplement. We don't take supplements in macrobiotics."

The problem was that Super Blue Green Algae came in a capsule. People on a macrobiotic health regimen had no problem with algae, per se. They consumed nori, kelp, wakame, and hijiki with gusto, all of which were forms of algae. But, by stuffing its algae into a capsule, Cell Tech had made it look like a pill, which is taboo in the macrobiotic world.

Showshawme did his best to convince Kim that all she had to do was pour the algae out of the capsule, and then it was no more of a "supplement" than a plate of hijiki. But common sense played little role in this clash of ideologies. If Showshawme wanted to win over the macrobiotic community, he had his work cut out for him.

The Pest Effect

For the next few weeks, Showshawme called Kim every day. Although she was irritated at first, Showshawme would often get her laughing with his zany sense of humor. It got to the point where Kim's boyfriend was starting to get upset.

"I never let up," says Showshawme. "I knew that she had connections all over the country and that would be a good thing for the business. I also knew that she would like the algae if she would only give it a chance."

At last, just to get rid of him, Kim made an offer. She would meet with him for an hour and try the algae. If she didn't like it, Showshawme would never bother her again.

A Major Convert

For 23 days, Kim ate four to six algae capsules per day. She felt nothing. Showshawme urged her to try more.

Eight capsules per day did the trick. Kim experienced a burst of energy. As the days went by, she found that her attention span for tedious administrative work had dramatically improved. Kim no longer had to take frequent breaks and consequently worked faster, harder, and more effectively.

"When you deal with macrobiotic counselors," comments Sue Grigsby, a Double Diamond distributor in Showshawme's downline, "you find that they think they know everything. Selling them on the algae was a real toughie. But Showshawme was smart to get them involved. In the end, it was the macrobiotic community that really set this business up."

To this day, a few macrobiotic purists remain who refuse to ingest encapsulated algae. But Kim Bright Cassano's influence was sufficient to win over several key opinion leaders in the macrobiotic field. At this writing, Showshawme estimates that her downline numbers more than 250,000.

AN OLD FRIEND

The "live-food" faction was almost as impregnable as the macrobiotic bloc. In the 1970s, author Victor Kulvinskas had written a book called *Survival into the 21st Century,* in which he popularized the notion that only "live" foods, such as fresh-grown alfalfa sprouts and wheat grass, contained proper nutrition. To Kulvinskas's followers, dried algae in capsules was "dead" and therefore useless.

Showshawme had one great advantage in attacking this market. Back in 1975, he had befriended Kulvinskas and even worked for him for a while. After *Survival into the 21st Century* came out, Showshawme had called up Kulvinskas—who lived in a neighboring Connecticut town—and offered his services to help promote the live-food diet. He set up seminars for Kulvinskas and spent a few years packing books and working at his publishing business. Showshawme used this connection now to approach Kulvinskas about his Cell Tech business. But the first approaches were discouraging.

Wear 'em Down

"Victor was so convinced that wheat grass and sprouts were the best foods on the planet," says Showshawme, "that he didn't want to hear about anything else. It took me a year and a half to convince him to sign up with Cell Tech."

Showshawme pestered Kulvinskas with stories about other peoples' success with the algae. He also pitched him on the great business opportunity of becoming a Cell Tech distributor.

"He told me he finally signed up just to get rid of me," Showshawme admits. "I pestered him until his resistance broke down."

A Shrewd Deal

But Showshawme had also shrewdly made Kulvinskas an offer he couldn't refuse. He had promised Kulvinskas that he would never have to pitch the business to anyone. Showshawme would do all the selling for him, as long as Kulvinskas would supply the leads.

This was a brilliant strategy. Kulvinskas reached thousands of health food enthusiasts through the lecture circuit. Now, whenever he gave a lecture, he talked about the Cell Tech algae and gave Showshawme's phone number. People interested in following up called Showshawme. Kulvinskas's downline grew with little or no effort on his part.

"Normally, I don't sign people up under another person," says Showshawme. "But, in Victor's case, I made an exception. Nowadays, he's a lot more independent. But he needed that jump start when he was just beginning."

A SLEEPER

For the first ten years, Cell Tech was a sleeper. It grew to only 30,000 distributors by 1992. Most were product users, not business builders. Indeed, the vast majority of Cell Tech distributors, at that time, tended to look upon moneymaking as a vice.

"People from other network marketing companies would laugh at us," says Showshawme. "We didn't have a lot of slick advertising, slick videos, and marketing seminars. It was a mom-and-pop type of company. We attracted the sort of people who wore Birkenstock sandals and ate granola. We couldn't attract the heavy hitters, because a lot of us were afraid to talk about money or promote it as a business."

Momentum

When the change hit, it came so suddenly that it took even Showshawme by surprise. First came the Green Wave—an explosion of interest in natural foods and herbal healing in the late 1980s. Wave Three followed soon after. Like hundreds of other network marketing companies across the nation, Cell Tech introduced videos, audiotapes, and programmatic sales training that standardized and simplified prospecting for ordinary people. The impact was immediate and astonishing. In three years, the company grew tenfold—and Showshawme's personal income with it.

"It's growing all the time now," says Showshawme. "Cell Tech grew 350 percent just in the last year."

The "M" Word

Cell Tech distributors are no longer afraid of uttering the "M" word, according to Showshawme. Money has become a major draw for a whole new breed of Cell Tech recruits: white-collar professionals attracted by the business opportunity rather than by hippie ideals.

"We're getting corporate people at an incredible rate now," says Showshawme. "We're attracting Wall Street people and business owners who are millionaires already."

Today, at the age of 44, Showshawme regularly prospects doctors and lawyers who make less money than he.

"Even millionaires that I've met are envious of my lifestyle," says Showshawme. "They have tons of money, but they have no time. Time freedom is a valuable thing. It means having the time to do whatever I choose in life. A lot of wealthy people have never even heard of that. They don't even know what it means."

Untold Abundance

Nowadays, Showshawme enjoys swimming in his private, chlorine-free pool and taking frequent vacations to the Caribbean. It's been a long time since he's felt guilty about having money. Showshawme has come to realize that prosperity complements, rather than conflicts, with his spiritual ideals. Indeed, one of his chief pleasures these days is donating to Cell Tech's humanitarian projects around the world.

"This planet will be a much better place if more people have financial abundance in their lives," he observes. "There will be less scarcity and more freedom. If people aren't worrying about where they're going to get their next meal or how they're going to pay their rent, there will be more opening up of people's hearts and sharing with one another."

IT'S NOT WHAT YOU KNOW—IT'S WHO YOU KNOW

Curled up in his mildewed tent in the Hawaiian rain forest, Showshawme appeared to be one of the least influential people on earth. Yet, even then, he possessed the potential to accomplish mighty deeds. Showshawme had no college degree. But he had an intimate knowledge of a particular subculture, knowledge that enabled him to pinpoint and recruit crucial opinion leaders with wide circles of influence.

Back in the early 1980s, nobody cared very much about the New Age subculture, save a few herbal tea manufacturers. But through the magic of MLM, Showshawme transmuted his network of aging hippies into a gold mine of resourcefulness and profit. No matter who you are, where you're from, or how you were educated, you too have access to hidden networks unknown and inaccessible to others. Find a product and a company that caters to their needs, and, like Showshawme, you can zero in on the "big fish" who will bring astonishing growth to your downline.

"I'm an example of a person who probably had more obstacles than most," says Showshawme. "But, with the help of a few key people, I was able to break through those obstacles and achieve my goals."

Chapter 7

AUTO-PROSPECTING

I 've got some great news," said the message on Donna Colson's voice-mail. "FreeLife has been named company of the month in *Moneymakers' Monthly!* As most of you know, that newspaper reaches thousands of people, so I think we can get some pretty good leads out of this."

Donna was excited. This was important news indeed. Nevertheless, Donna didn't bother reaching for a pad or pencil. She knew that taking notes was unnecessary.

"We're taking out a huge co-op ad in the same issue," the recorded voice continued. "It'll be the centerfold for the entire paper. So if you want to participate in this co-op, just Voice-Tel me back. The spots are $500 apiece, on a first come, first served basis."

Sounds good, thought Donna. She reached out her finger and pressed "A" for "answer" on her telephone keypad—the only physical effort required from Donna throughout the entire process.

"Hi, Colli," she said into the voice-mailbox. "This is Donna. Put me down for two of those $500 spots, will you?"

The Not-So-Cold Market

Donna Colson was working her "cold market." At one time, those were the two most fearsome words in the network marketer's vocabulary. Working your cold market meant stepping outside the warm cocoon of family and friends. It meant cold-calling strangers on the phone and enduring their hang-ups and nasty rejections. It meant setting up booths at trade shows. Sometimes it even meant accosting people on the street. The risk of failure was high and the emotional strain intense.

But today, Wave-Three technology has taken much of the cold out of cold markets. The newest "auto-prospecting" procedures have removed the need to talk to strangers—except, of course, when those strangers want to talk to you. Auto-prospecting systems screen your prospects in advance. They shield you from rejection, cut down your prospecting time, and allow you to channel your time, energy, and emotional reserves into the more fruitful task of working with your best leads.

Automated Advertising

Take Donna Colson. After placing her order for the ad co-op, her job was virtually done. Donna was free to go about her business. What little work remained was handled by Donna's sponsor, Colli Butler. Colli, for example, made all the arrangements for placing the ad in *Moneymakers' Monthly*. When prospects started responding to the ad and calling the 800 number, Colli took care of that too. All the messages came straight to Colli's voice-mailbox.

Even for Colli, the work was minimal. Each time a call came in, she would check her list of people participating in the ad co-op. Whoever was next on the list would get that particular lead. Let's say it was Donna Colson's turn on the list. The very next call that came in, Colli would reach out, push "G" for "give" on her touch-tone keypad, and then type in Donna Colson's Voice-Tel number. The message was immediately zapped to Donna's personal voice-mailbox. So, when Donna finally got around to checking her messages, she would hear something like:

"Hi, my name is Tom Smith. I saw your ad and I want to know more about FreeLife. Would you please send me some material at such-and-such address?"

That way, the only people Donna had to deal with were those who had already requested information. Through such "automated" ad co-ops placed in various publications, Donna and her downline receive a constant stream of positive leads each month. Such leads would have required hundreds of hours of cold-calling to gather by traditional methods.

The Gee-Whiz Factor

There are many forms of autoprospecting. The simplest and easiest version got its start in the late 1980s with the advent of mass video mailings. This simply means obtaining a mailing list, sending out packets of prospecting videos to everyone on the list, and then following up by phone.

When video prospecting first began, it benefited from the "Gee-Whiz" Factor that accompanies every new technology. VCRs were sufficiently new, at that time, so that most prospects who received a free video in the mail would tend to play it just for the thrill of seeing moving pictures issue forth from a magnetic tape cassette. Video and audio mailings are still highly effective auto-prospecting techniques, but the Gee-Whiz Factor has long since faded. Today, the psychological edge has moved to a new frontier: the Internet.

THE NEW FRONTIER

At a time when most high-profile Web sites are limping along with multimillion-dollar deficits, network marketers have emerged as "one of the few groups actually doing successful commercial business on the Internet," says John Fogg, founding editor of *Upline,* an MLM trade publication with a heavy online presence (http://www.up lineonline.com). "You've got people out there with down-lines of 1,500 to 2,000 distributors built solely online."

Every time you send a video or audiotape in the mail, you have to spend time and money. But a home page on the World Wide Web only has to be posted once. A home page is a sort of computerized display ad on the Internet that can even branch off to countless other pages for your company. People exploring the Web from their computers can come across your home page and peruse all your com-pany's pages at their leisure. There the page sits for a low monthly fee, advertising your business opportunity to mil-lions of potential recruits while providing a built-in e-mail link for immediate and direct responses from interested prospects.

Stan and Donna Colson are among those MLM pio-neers who have already managed to build an extensive downline via a Web site. An entire leg of their FreeLife organization is built from people recruited online. By automating much of the drudgery and tedium of cold-market prospecting, the Internet allows Stan Colson to participate, as an equal partner, in his wife's FreeLife business—despite the fact that he still holds a full-time job as a computer analyst.

"I'm basically a computer guy," says Stan, "so I man-age the Web site. Donna is a great phone closer, so I pass the leads on to her and she follows up."

Hard Work, Meager Rewards

Like many small business owners, the Colsons learned the hard way that self-employment can be a raw deal. In their quest for financial freedom, they tried running a stained-glass lamp shop, a candy store, a video service, a fudge cart in a local mall, and a small chain of computer dealerships.

The Colsons saved, scrounged, and sacrificed, living for eight years and raising two children in a windowless basement beneath their storefront. Despite all the risk and hard work, the Colsons never succeeded in raising their income over $50,000 per year. Most of the time, it was much lower. Yet, both of them had to work like dogs just to get that.

The Last Straw

For Stan Colson, the final straw came when he ended up running a small chain of three Apple computer stores. A mechanical engineer by training, Stan was an early enthusiast of personal computers. He thought selling computers would allow him to make money doing something he enjoyed. But Stan discovered that his private passion mixed poorly with the practical demands of running a business.

"I discovered that I'm the sort of person who just wants to be responsible for himself," says Stan. "I didn't want to worry about other people or have responsibility for payrolls. Even holding the reins on my store managers turned out to be more than I wanted to do."

The Delegation Myth

Stan had heard that delegation would make your job easier. But the more he delegated, the more his problems grew. At one point, Stan gave his managers free rein to buy inventory for their stores. For two of the stores, that seemed to work. But one of his managers would overextend himself every month, like clockwork, spending more money on inventory than he had taken in from sales.

"Every month, I'd have to run down to the bank with him and get a short-term loan until the receivables came in to pay it off," says Stan. "And I just got tired of doing that."

Eventually, Stan had had enough. He sold all three stores to their respective managers. Not surprisingly, the manager with the overspending problem immediately spent himself into bankruptcy. His store went under in six months.

"Unfortunately," says Stan, "I had financed that sale myself, so when he went bankrupt, I was left with some worthless paper."

The "Good Life"

Stan was tired. Twelve years of sleepless nights and 14-hour workdays was enough. With far more relief than regret, Stan finally gave up his dream of financial independence and got himself a "real" job, working as a computer analyst for the U.S. Department of Energy.

"I started living the good life," he says, "punching the clock, going in at 7:30 A.M., coming home at 4 P.M., and thinking, 'Man, this is the life.' When the clock strikes four, you can just forget about it, go home, and be with your family. I kind of liked that."

Unfortunately, Stan's honeymoon with the 40-hour work week was doomed from the start. When the first wave of government downsizing hit, Stan thought he was immune. But then two out of his group of six computer analysts unexpectedly got their pink slips.

"It woke me up," says Stan. "Those guys didn't even see it coming. It gave me the idea that maybe I'm not indispensable. It could happen to me."

Financial Pressures

To add to Stan's problems, financial pressures were building up. The Colsons' house was 13 years old and the appliances were all breaking down.

"We didn't know if Stan would have his job long, and we were afraid to spend money," says Donna. "The dishwasher, the refrigerator, and the dryer were busted, and I was washing dishes by hand and hanging things up to dry. We started renting out rooms to bring in extra money."

For a while, Donna worked in real estate. But she soon realized it wasn't for her.

"The life of a realtor is hard," says Donna. "You're constantly at everyone's beck and call. You lose your evenings and weekends. Everyone is your boss. I felt, at times, that I was literally going to have a nervous breakdown."

But quitting real estate provided only momentary relief. For the first time since Donna and Stan married, they were dependent on a single income. And Stan's job could vanish any day.

A Lifeline

It was right at that moment that the Colsons were thrown an unexpected lifeline. It happens that David Butler (whom we met in Chapter 5) is Donna Colson's brother. When David and Colli Butler started their FreeLife business, they had pledged not to involve friends or family until they were absolutely sure the company was going to make it. Both of them had experienced too many disappointments in their MLM career to want to inflict such hardship on loved ones. But after several successful months in the business, David and Colli were ready to talk. That summer, they came out to visit the Colsons for two weeks.

"We weren't exactly sure what sort of business they were doing, but we could see that they were making money," Donna recalls. "So we were just kind of feeling around, asking them what they were up to. We didn't plan on doing it with them, of course, because we knew it was network marketing and we'd had some bad experiences with that industry. But still, we found out that they were making something like $10,000 a month at that point, and we couldn't help being curious."

A Part-Time Mentality

Donna Colson's tarnished image of network marketing came from her own past brushes with the industry. Like most MLMers, Donna had a part-time mentality. She had no interest in working seven days per week to build a business. Unfortunately, during the Wave-Two era, when Donna had first dabbled in MLM, few companies catered to part-timers.

In one company, Donna had signed up a couple of people and sold them about $200 worth of product. But, at the end of the month, she received no commission. Donna called up her sponsor to ask why.

"You haven't met your group volume yet," her sponsor explained.

Donna then learned that she had to move at least $500 worth of product each month before she could make one cent in commission.

"I had assumed that if I sold some product, I'd make some money," says Donna. "But it didn't work that way. I felt a little bit cheated, especially since I'd paid a $20 sign-up fee. All I wanted was a little part-time income. There was no way I was going to work hard enough to sell $500 worth of product every month. So I dropped out of the program."

A Program for the Little Guy

What Donna didn't realize, however, was that a revolution had occurred during the years since her last MLM experience—the Wave-Three Revolution. As she listened to David and Colli Butler, Donna slowly began to realize how much the industry was changing.

"In FreeLife," says Donna, "if just one person signs up and buys something from you, you make a small commission."

Like other Wave-Three companies, FreeLife also offered a drop-shipping program. In past companies, Donna had been forced to stockpile the product. She still had $300 worth of unsold skin cream left over from one abortive venture 18 years before! But, in FreeLife, you didn't have to stockpile inventory at all. Your retail customers order directly from the company through an 800 number, using a credit card if they wish. If they wanted to buy at wholesale, they just filled out a form. There was no entry fee to become a distributor.

"I saw that people didn't have to bug each other," says Donna. "I didn't have to bug you to get the products, and you didn't have to bug me if you wanted to buy them. It really seemed doable. And with Dr. Earl Mindell, the number one nutritionist in the world, behind the products, how could we fail? We figured we might as well give it a try."

Geometric Growth

In the beginning, Donna worked her FreeLife business with little help from her husband. Stan had his hands full with his job. But, as the weeks went by, Stan couldn't help noticing her progress.

"Her first week in the business, Donna signed up one person and got $4.10 in commissions," Stan recalls. "But the next month, she got $200. The following month, it was over $400, and then it jumped to $800. Well, I'd taken enough math to know what would happen if this thing kept doubling every month. At that point, all I could say was, 'Hey, honey, how can I help?'"

SERVICE BEFORE ADVERTISING

As a computer professional, Stan had spent enough time surfing the World Wide Web to see its potential as a prospecting device. He also felt he had a good handle on its flaws and weaknesses.

"Most of the World Wide Web is like a big Sears catalog," says Stan. "It's just one advertising come-on after another. You get tired of it real soon."

Stan knew that the Gee-Whiz Factor would keep people surfing the Web only so long. The Web sites with staying power would be those that provided useful information and service. Stan figured that a Web site devoted to the nutritional teachings of Dr. Earl Mindell would be a much bigger draw than a recruitment come-on for Free-Life. So he set out to create a *Readers' Digest*–type version of Dr. Mindell's writings.

"I did a series of mini-articles based on Dr. Mindell's published research," says Stan, "and linked them all together so that, if you hit one of the articles, at the bottom you'd find a shopping list of all the other articles."

People searching the Web for such topics as "Dr. Earl Mindell," "antiaging," or "nutrition" would find their way quickly to one or the other of Stan's home pages. Once there, they could select various hyperlinks—highlighted text that moves you from one Web page to another when you click your cursor over it. No one had to be bothered with the

MLM opportunity unless they deliberately selected the FreeLife hyperlink. It was purely a matter of choice.

Short, Concise Pages

Stan knew from experience that nothing is more irritating to a Web surfer than having to sit for ten minutes waiting for the computer to download a home page that has been overstuffed with text and graphics.

"I decided to make each individual page short and concise," says Stan. "I figured that it's better to have four to five pages linked together than a single large page."

Having more pages also increases the chances that people will hit your Web site, provided you register each page separately with a search engine—an online service that allows Web users to type in words or phrases and get a list of Web sites containing those phrases.

Fast-Loading Graphics

Because they use more information, graphics are major culprits in slowing down Web pages. Yet, a page without graphics is a boring page. Stan found two ways to keep the graphic bottleneck to a minimum without sacrificing graphics entirely.

First, he limited each graphic to 20 kilobytes or less. This can be done by cropping the graphic, shrinking it, or switching it to a format that offers less resolution and therefore lower density of information. This would happen, for example, if you took a graphic that had been scanned in as a "JPEG" file and transformed it to a "GIF" file. Stan found that he could thus cut the loading time for graphics down to 30 seconds or less—the critical threshold where a Web surfer's attention starts to wander.

Reuse Your Graphics

The second way Stan discovered to cut down on graphics bottlenecks was to reuse the same graphic on different pages of his Web site, almost like a logo. "Browsers" (software programs that enable computers to locate and read Web pages and search the Internet), such as Netscape or Mosaic need to load a particular graphic only once—the first time they encounter it during a session. For the remainder of the session, the graphic remains stored in memory and can be reproduced instantly as needed. So every subsequent time the browser encounters that same graphic, the computer pops it back onto the page without a lengthy downloading procedure.

Stan chose a photograph of Dr. Mindell as his "logo" image. By reproducing it in different sizes and different positions on the various pages of his Web site, he was able to create an illusion of variety while reusing the same graphic again and again.

The Top of the Page Is the Most Important

Even with all this streamlining, the very best of Web pages will still take a few seconds to load. During that time, the Web surfer has to sit patiently and stare at the screen. Since most browsers load from the top down, Stan realized that prospects would spend most of their time looking just at the very top of the page. By the time the rest of it loaded, many would be so tired of waiting that they probably wouldn't bother to scroll down to the rest of the page. Instead, they might just click over to someone else's home page. Stan realized that he had to design his pages so that the top of the page alone would convey the essence of his message, through concise headlines, subheads, pictures, and captions.

"There's got to be something in the top of that page," says Stan, "that tells them right away what they're looking at."

Use Search Engines

Of course, just posting your page on the Internet isn't enough. If you want to get "traffic"—a steady stream of Web surfers "hitting" your site—you need to let people know it's out there. For those willing to pay, there are many venues on the Internet for advertising your Web page. But the most effective way to publicize your site is entirely free of charge.

You simply need to get it listed with a search engine. This is a tedious and time-consuming process that involves filling out online submission forms for each and every available search engine. When Stan first posted his site, there were nearly 200 search engines available on the World Wide Web. Even after you fill out the forms, not every search engine will automatically list your Web site. Some will examine it first to see if they consider it worthy of a listing. The process can take weeks.

"At first, I tried to register all of my pages in every search engine available," says Stan. "But it took about ten days to get them all registered. Now, when I add new pages, I just list them in the Big Ten search engines. If you do a Yahoo search (a search for particular word or phrase, using the well-known search engine Yahoo, at http://www.yahoo.com) and look at the search engines listed at the bottom of the page, you'll get a pretty good idea who the big ones are."

Stan found that from the time his page was listed, it took about three to four weeks before people started finding it and sending e-mail responses.

Save Time, Save Money

Of the various auto-prospecting methods available, Web sites are clearly the most efficient, in time and money. Once your home page is posted, maintenance is minimal. The biggest time investment occurs at the beginning. Stan, for example, took about 60 hours to post his first dozen pages. Since then, he's been adding a few pages per week, spending four to five hours on each page. At this printing, he currently has about 150 pages posted at http://www.ncw.net/alpha/freelife.html.

Compared to the costs of print advertising and direct mailings, Web sites are a steal. If you design the site yourself (and there's really no need to hire a designer for a simple Web site), your biggest cost will be your monthly fee to a local provider—a company in your area that stores your Web page on a server, which is a computer that is hooked up 24 hours per day to the Internet.

"It cost us $25 to have a monthly Internet connect and $50 additional to be a commercial site, which is defined as a site where you sell something," says Stan. "So I pay $75 per month total."

CAVEAT EMPTOR

Stan cautions newcomers against enrolling in Internet seminars.

"A lot of them try to front-end load you with a bunch of their services," he says. "I know one lady and her husband who signed up for a program that promised to train you and get you set up with your own Web site for $3,500. For several months afterward, they were busy taking classes, reading manuals, and finding out how to do everything. It seemed to take an awful long time."

Stan points out that most local Internet providers will give you a free Web page and walk you through the basics of setting up your site with no extra charge. Many will even scan in graphics for you or recommend a local service where you can have it done.

"For people who are serious about doing business on the Web, I think the focus should be more on the content of the pages than on the actual nuts and bolts of how to get it online," says Stan. "The best way to learn the nuts and bolts is to just start doing it."

A good service for beginners is America Online, which not only provides 10 megabytes of free Web space to every subscriber (a huge quantity!) but also offers free on-line Internet classes and a 24-hour bulletin board (called The Web Diner) that allows you to pose questions to Internet experts and receive detailed technical assistance in getting your page online. This author, for example, with no special knowledge of computers, created a Wave-Three home page on America Online (http://members.aol.com/wave3page/wave3.html) that is currently enjoying a high level of traffic.

TRIAL AND ERROR

Over time, Stan and Donna evolved an efficient methodology for Internet prospecting. But they made a lot of mistakes along the way.

"At first, I responded to every query and sent back an e-mail telling them about the products," says Stan. "But I ended up sending a lot of packets out and didn't get a whole lot of people signing up."

Donna kept detailed files on every prospect. She would print out each incoming e-mail and each response that she and Stan made to it, stapling them together and keeping them alphabetized in a file. Whenever they mailed an audiotape to a prospect, Donna moved that prospect's paperwork to a different file.

"I noticed that the file of people who received audiotapes was just getting bigger and bigger, but they weren't signing up," Donna recalls. "We couldn't call them, because we didn't have their phone numbers. So we would e-mail them, asking if they wanted any further help. But they wouldn't answer. That's when I realized these people weren't really interested. We were just wasting our money by sending them packets."

Freebie Scavengers

Some of these false leads may have been people who legitimately reviewed the material and rejected the opportunity. But Donna thinks most were Internet freebie scavengers—people who surf the Web, compulsively sending away for every free item they can get, whether or not they need or want it.

"What we realized is happening," says Donna, "is that people are out there cruising the Internet saying, 'Wow, you can get all kinds of free stuff out here. This is fun!' So when you have a page that says 'Call or write for our free audiotape,' they just click 'reply' and say, 'Send me your free tape.' They don't care what it is, as long as it's free."

Prescreening

Donna developed a procedure for screening out the scavengers. Now, whenever she gets a request for a tape, she e-mails the respondent and says, "I'll be happy to send you our free tape, but first we need your telephone number, because we like to follow up with people after they have a chance to look over the materials we send them."

Real prospects will provide their phone numbers willingly. Freebie vultures and tire kickers will generally shy away.

"I very often end up writing two or three e-mails," says Donna. "First, they write and request the tape. Then I write back and say, 'First, send me your address and phone number.' Then maybe they'll send their address, but no phone number. We just keep going back and forth. Only when I get the phone number will I stick a packet in the mail. If they're willing to give us a phone number, that's a big feat. It means they don't mind being contacted."

A 25 PERCENT SIGN-UP RATE

The screening procedure proved critical. It kicked off a Butterfly Effect that quickly put Stan and Donna's Internet business over the top. Only two weeks after they started screening, their recruitment rate skyrocketed. At this printing, they're getting 60 to 80 e-mails per day, about half of which are requests for information about the business or products. Of that number, the Colsons are signing up about 20 percent.

"They're coming in by the hordes now," says Donna. "Twenty-five percent is a very good sign-up rate. In the past, I've spent fortunes putting ads in our local newspaper where you'll get maybe two responses and only one signs up."

According to Stan, the number of queries per day doubled after the first month. He routinely gets queries from every state in the Union and from countries as diverse as Sweden and Zaire.

A "Doable" Business

"We're making about $4,000 per month now," says Donna, "and I expect we'll hit five figures by the end of the year."

Not all of the Colsons' recruits come from auto-prospecting. Donna does much of her recruiting the old-fashioned way, through meetings and warm markets. But for Stan, the Internet has proved critical to his MLM career. It enables him to take a dynamic role in the FreeLife business, even while keeping a full-time job. It also lets him exploit his technical skills while avoiding those areas—such as phone solicitation—where he is weaker. Auto-prospecting has made MLM doable for Stan Colson. For thousands of others like him, it has opened a door to realistic and profitable self-employment that had long remained closed.

Chapter 8

FIND THE RIGHT GOALS

P eople are not lazy," says personal development author Anthony Robbins. "They simply have impotent goals—that is, goals that do not inspire them." Every network marketer knows the frustration of trying to motivate "lazy" people. You spend hours with them on the phone. You drag them to seminars. You inspire them with visions of wealth and leisure. You provoke them with fears of poverty. But nothing seems to work. Year after year, they stay in the same rut, refusing to make the simplest moves that you know would propel their downlines into high-speed growth.

Different Goals

You may be dealing with a person whose goals in life are different from yours. In fact, as Anthony Robbins points out, there's no such thing as a truly "lazy" person. There are only people who haven't yet seized upon a sufficiently compelling reason to offer their total commitment.

People who are quick to enthuse often lose their steam just as quickly. Like the hare in the old fable, they jump to an early lead only to yield their place later to the plodding tortoise. But those who take months or even years to build up a steady momentum can be like 90-ton locomotives. Once in motion, they are unstoppable.

Cherish your lazy people. Ask them questions and listen carefully to their answers. Mine them as you would an untapped vein of gold. If you can learn the secret to their inner hearts, you will open doors to unexpected riches. Sooner than you think, your lazy people may one day reveal themselves as the steady tortoise who beats everyone to the finish line.

A PLODDING TORTOISE

For years, Bill King frustrated his sponsors. No one could figure out how to light his fire. Bill used all the products and loved them. He brushed with Oxyfresh toothpaste and dental gel, rinsed with Oxyfresh mouthwash, popped Oxyfresh breath mints in his mouth through the day, and flushed his teeth with the Oxycare 3000 Oral Irrigator. His wife, Susan, used Oxyfresh's "Aiyana" line of organic skin treatments, body lotion, and shampoo. She even did her laundry with Oxyfresh natural detergent.

Indeed, the King household was a veritable showcase of Oxyfresh products, while Bill and Susan were among the company's most loyal distributors. Even when money was tight, they managed more than once to scrape up the hotel fees and transportation costs for Oxyfresh events out of town.

Yet, year after year, Bill's downline stagnated. He'd recruit a couple of people here, sell a little product there. But, for a man of Bill's talents and abilities, his sponsors expected far more. No one could figure out how to motivate Bill King to take that bold first step down the road of total commitment.

A Perfectionist

The problem was, Bill's sponsors weren't looking in the right place. The clue to his motivation lay in plain sight.

All they needed to do was look at what Bill did for a living every day.

Bill ran a dental lab. He made ceramic crowns and bridges for dentists. Back in college, Bill had dreamed of being a dentist himself. But when he couldn't get into dentistry school, he decided that being a dental technician was the next best thing. Though he had fallen short of his dream, Bill made up for it by being the best dental technician he knew how to be.

Every prosthetic he made was hand-ground to a perfect fit. At times, Bill tried to hire assistants to ease some of the workload. But no one seemed to put the same care and diligence into the work as Bill. He went through one assistant after another. In the end, Bill ended up doing most of the work himself.

"It wasn't uncommon for me to get up at six in the morning and work 12, 14, sometimes even 18 hours a day," says Bill.

A Giving Spirit

Bill knew that he didn't have to do such a perfect job. In fact, he saw that a lot of competing labs got by with inferior work. By cutting corners on quality, they could produce more prostheses at a cheaper price. Bill lost a lot of business to these cut-rate labs, because so many dentists bought on price rather than quality.

Yet Bill never considered cutting corners himself. No matter how much it cost him in time and money, he kept his standards high. Sometimes Bill struggled a little to pay his mortgage on time and to keep his five children clothed and fed. But each time he shipped a crown or a bridge to one of his customers, Bill felt a warm glow of satisfaction in his heart, because he knew that some patient out there in some dentist's office was about to get the very best dental prosthetic that human hands could make. And that's what Bill King lived for.

Thankless Toil

One day, fate played a cruel trick on Bill. Through a bizarre series of mishaps, Bill suddenly lost four major accounts in the space of six months.

One of his clients had a stroke and lost his dental practice. Another suffered a heart attack. A third dentist got married, sold his practice, and left town. The dentist who took over his practice chose a lab with lower prices than Bill's. Then came the final blow. A man whom Bill had trained set up a competing lab and lured away one of Bill's best clients—a dentist who just happened to be the man's son-in-law.

"In a matter of six months," says Bill, "I had lost about 40 percent of my business."

Bill struggled back to his feet the same way he always had in the past—through hard work and long hours. But he was 39 years old now, and the work was starting to take its toll.

The Writing on the Wall

When he was young and hale, Bill never thought twice about working 18-hour days. But as the years crept by, Bill's punishing regimen had begun to catch up with him.

First, he developed a chronic soreness in one shoulder from the endless, repetitive hand-grinding. Then, one day, he noticed a strange numbness in his hands and a tingling sensation similar to what you feel when your hand falls asleep. Sometimes, the tingling and numbness got so bad, Bill couldn't even work.

"You've got carpal tunnel syndrome," Bill's doctor told him.

Carpal tunnel syndrome is a debilitating condition afflicting people who do repetitive work with their hands. There was no real cure, said the doctor. As long as Bill kept using his hands to make dental prostheses, the condition was bound to get a little worse all the time.

"That's when I started to see the writing on the wall," says Bill.

A Ray of Hope

Not long after that, Bill received an unexpected visitor at his dental lab in Salt Lake City. Her name was Roxie Hayes. Roxie was dynamic, attractive, professional, and well-dressed. She introduced herself as a representative of Oxyfresh, a company that made a full line of dental hygiene products. Whipping out a tube of Oxyfresh toothpaste, she suggested Bill try a taste of it.

"You're in the dental field, and I think this is something that you might have an interest in," she said.

Roxie then dabbed a little of the toothpaste on Bill's hand and told him to rub it on his front teeth. Bill was amazed at the great taste. His gums tingled with freshness.

"Now how would you like your whole mouth to feel like that every day?" asked Roxie with a smile.

Low Pressure

Bill had to agree that the toothpaste was pretty good. But he was less than pleased by what Roxie said next.

"There's a business opportunity with this," said Roxie. "Oxyfresh is a network marketing company."

Oh no, not this again, thought Bill. In the last few years, Bill had tried to supplement his income by dabbling with several different MLM companies. In the end, it always ended the same way—with a lot of people trying to pressure him into spending more time, money, and effort on the business than he could afford.

Nevertheless, Bill had to admit there was something different about Roxie. Her approach was not pushy at all. She seemed far more professional than the others. And she was thoroughly confident in her products. Roxie gave Bill a small, travel-sized tube of Oxyfresh toothpaste and told him to think about it as long as he liked.

The Follow-up

Bill loved the toothpaste. It left his mouth feeling as fresh and clean as if he had just gotten a professional cleaning at the dentist's.

"When we ran out of Oxyfresh toothpaste and went back to our old brand, it just about gagged me," says Bill. "I couldn't believe how bad it tasted in comparison with Oxyfresh. So I decided I was going to use the toothpaste whether or not I ever worked the business."

As the weeks went by, Roxie continued working on Bill and Susan. She pointed out how many Oxyfresh distributors were dental professionals and what a great prospect base Bill would have among his colleagues and clients. She also briefed the Kings on the company's unique history and management strength.

An All-Star Team

Only four years before, Roxie told them, Oxyfresh had been just one more struggling MLM startup on the verge of bankruptcy. Distributors were leaving in droves. Sales were plummeting. In a last, desperate move, the company turned to Richard Brooke, a successful network marketer from a rival company.

They offered Brooke the presidency of Oxyfresh and a controlling share of the stock if he could turn it around. Within a year, Brooke and his team had worked a miracle. They instituted a new corporate culture based on professionalism and high ethical standards. In the first four years of Brooke's leadership, Oxyfresh increased its sales from $1.3 million to over $12 million. Today, it is one of only a handful of network marketing companies with the staying power to have survived and prospered into its second decade.

The Big Question

Bill and Susan were soon enrolled as Oxyfresh distributors. But it wasn't long before Bill found himself slipping into the familiar pattern he had found with his past network marketing businesses. He began each week with ambitious goals. But as the week wore on, reality would set in. With the demands of his dental lab increasing all the time, Bill simply couldn't spare the time and energy to focus on Oxyfresh.

Bill had heard all the pep talks and motivational speeches. But none of them seemed to address his primary concern. If Bill listened to Roxie and devoted the kind of time to Oxyfresh that she wanted, how could he continue to maintain the high quality and production volume of his dental business? Neither Roxie nor any other network marketer had ever offered Bill what he felt was a reasonable answer to this question.

A Vicious Circle

Nor did the problem seem inclined to just go away of its own accord. On the contrary, the harder Bill worked at his dental business, the more it seemed to demand of him. At times, he felt that he was caught in a vicious circle, working more and more to earn less and less.

"My costs were always rising," he says. "But every time I raised my prices, the dentists would complain, and I'd lose an account. Then I'd have to go out and spend more time recruiting a new account. With all that going on, Oxyfresh was a pretty low priority."

A Rude Awakening

One day, about a year after joining the Oxyfresh business, Bill got a shock. Roxie announced she was leaving. Because of some pressing family issues, she was taking a lengthy sabbatical from Oxyfresh.

Until that moment, Bill had never realized how dependent he had become on Roxie's hectoring. Though he seldom took her advice, the mere fact that she was there, encouraging, pestering, and pushing him to look beyond that next order for a dental prosthetic was mysteriously comforting. In the absence of any strong outside ambitions of his own, Bill was often secretly glad that he had Roxie to dream and set goals for him.

Now that crutch was about to be yanked away. From now on, Bill would have to set his own goals and dream his own dreams. He found this a far more frightening prospect than he would have expected.

A New Coach

Roxie urged Bill to pursue a relationship with her sponsor, a man named Roland Fox, who happened to be the number one distributor in Oxyfresh. At first, Bill balked. He was intimidated by Roland's wealth and by his reputation as a go-getter. On the one hand, Bill couldn't believe a man of Roland's stature would waste time with a small fry like him. On the other hand, Bill wasn't even sure he wanted that kind of attention. He imagined it would be a little bit like enlisting in the Marines under a tough and merciless drill sergeant. Bill wasn't sure he was ready to make that leap.

The Leap

But deep in his heart, Bill knew he had to do something. Without a substantial second income, he was betting his family's security on an increasingly risky dental business and on his own shaky health. Bill resolved to make the call. But it was easier said than done.

"The phone became a 600-pound weight," Bill remembers. "I sat there for two hours, picking up the phone, starting to dial the number, then putting it down again. I was just plain scared."

In the end, when Bill could no longer tell which was worse—the agony of indecision or the fear of making the call—he finally forced himself to dial the number.

A Team Player

Bill was pleasantly surprised to find that Roland Fox was warm and cordial on the phone. Roland offered immediately to come out and work with Bill for five days, to train him and develop some momentum in his business. At first, Bill assumed Roland would want to be put up in a fancy hotel and supplied with a rental car. But Roland had other plans.

"I'll just come and stay with you," he said.

Bill's modest house was in a chronic state of disorder from the demands of five children and a full-fledged dental lab complete with tools and equipment. His wife flew into a panic when Bill told her about their unexpected VIP guest.

"We made up all this stuff in our heads about how he would judge us and look down on us because of our circumstances," Bill recalls. "But, it wasn't like that at all. Roland was just a great person. When he got here, my kids took right to him. He took right to the kids. He just fit right in. He was a normal human being."

Roland Fox was a team player. During the five days of training, he impressed upon Bill and Susan the importance of getting hooked into the Oxyfresh network. By the time Roland left, Bill and Susan had made many promises and commitments. But none proved more important than their promise to attend the next Leadership Training seminar at company headquarters in Spokane, Washington.

The Breakthrough

Although Susan's mother lived in Spokane, Roland urged them to stay in the hotel with the other participants. He wanted them to get the full experience of living and interacting with the Oxyfresh team.

During the seminar, Bill and Susan made many friends and imbibed inspiration from the company's top movers and shakers. But, for Bill, the most memorable event occurred when he was asked to take his turn introducing himself to the group.

A Small Dream with a Big Punch

During their introduction, all participants were asked to imagine that their financial worries were suddenly over. Now that cost was no longer an issue, what would they most like to do in life? Participants were asked to share their dreams with the group.

As many times as Bill had asked himself this question, he realized at the seminar that he'd never managed to formulate a clear answer for it. Bill wasn't the sort of person who dreamed about fancy cars and luxurious mansions. What he enjoyed most was doing his work well and spending time with his family. As Bill stood to address the group, he found himself thinking about pleasant afternoons he'd spent fly-fishing with his family. He thought of the cool water sloshing about his boots, the springy feel of the rod, the silver flash of a fish leaping in the stream. Then Bill heard his own voice speaking, as if from far away.

"I guess what I'd really like most," said Bill, "is, just once in my life, to take my wife and go fly-fishing down in New Zealand."

When he took his seat afterward, Bill was almost surprised at the smiles and nods of encouragement that met him from all around the room. He was embarrassed by the modesty of his dream. It seemed inadequate compared with the lavish ambitions some other participants had expressed. Yet, Bill knew that he had spoken from the deepest and most hidden recesses of his heart. The dream he had uttered was unmistakably and absolutely his own. Its magic would resonate in Bill's life for years to come.

Massive Action

Under Roland Fox's tutelage, Bill's feeble downline at last began stirring to life. Through an exercise of almost superhuman discipline, Bill managed to squeeze two to five hours of consistent Oxyfresh prospecting into each busy week. Soon he was earning $1,700 to $2,000 per month in commissions. But Bill knew he could do better. He knew that he had yet to stretch his prospecting muscles to that pinnacle of exertion that Oxyfresh president Richard Brooke called "massive action."

"Think of it as pushing a stalled car over the crest of a hill," Brooke would say. "You have to keep pressure on in the beginning until you crest the hill."

Bill King had been pushing his "car" up that hill for a long time. But he knew he had a long way to go before reaching the crest. Bill simply couldn't sacrifice more time than he already had. To do that would mean letting his dental business slip. And Bill could never, ever allow that to happen. All the riches and freedom in the world could never bribe Bill King to allow one single prosthetic to ship from his lab that was less than perfectly made. For it was quality and service—not money—that fired Bill King's soul.

Electronic Leverage

Just at that moment, Bill's daughter came through with a suggestion that was to change his life. She sent him an article from college about the Internet. Typically, Bill allowed the article to sit unread for several months. But his daughter wouldn't let the subject drop.

"She hammered me pretty good," says Bill. "I finally read it, and things just began to click."

Bill knew next to nothing about the Internet. But the article sparked his imagination. It instilled in his mind a slender hope that maybe, just maybe there was a way to leverage his prospecting time into "massive action"— without sacrificing on the quality or productivity of his dental work.

A Transformation

Fired by this hope, Bill underwent a sudden and remarkable transformation. The shy man who had tiptoed uncertainly through his Oxyfresh business for four long years vanished overnight. Now another Bill King took his place, one who seldom showed his face in public but who had ruled his dental lab with an iron fist for over 20 years. This was the uncompromising perfectionist who had fired assistant after assistant from his dental lab, without mercy. This was the man who had ignored doctors' warnings, rising each morning at dawn to grind and punish his flesh, in defiance of the crippling effects of carpal tunnel syndrome.

Service—The Ultimate Juice

What fueled Bill's extraordinary transformation was the same "juice" that had kept him chained to his dental lab for 20 years—an obsession with *service*. Instinctively, Bill had grasped a principle of the Internet that only a few really appreciate—that it gives without asking in return, that its fundamental nature lends itself to a generous outpouring of free service and information, that, in the right hands, a well-layered Web site can become the ultimate vehicle for feeding a marketplace ever more hungry for richness and satisfaction beyond the ordinary.

"Through all the leadership courses and trainings, I did a lot of self-searching," says Bill. "And the thing that kept coming up was my need to contribute and make a difference. That's what really juices me. It's not just building my own organization but doing something that's going to help other people. I saw the Internet as a way to accomplish that."

A Big Vision

For years, Bill had felt like a spectator in Oxyfresh, watching the big parade from afar. Now, without prelude or warning, it was suddenly Bill who was leading the brass band.

With startling clarity, Bill seized upon a vision that no one else seemed to grasp. He foresaw a grand new direction for the company that could benefit every distributor and launch Oxyfresh into the forefront of 21st-century network marketing.

"I had a gut feeling that the World Wide Web was not going to go away," Bill recalls. "I knew it was going to build and develop into something big."

Salesman Extraordinaire

Only recently, Bill had sat frozen in his office for two hours, trembling at the very thought of calling Roland Fox on the phone. Now it was Bill who took the lead and told Roland what to do.

"I don't want to do anything with computers," Roland groused when Bill first pitched him on the Internet idea. But Bill wouldn't take no for an answer. His newfound enthusiasm had transformed him into a salesman extraordinaire. Within a short time, Bill had won over not only Roland but even a skeptical Richard Brooke. He gained Oxyfresh's permission to go online with a massive corporate Web site, in which potentially hundreds of distributors could participate on a cooperative basis.

The Frontier of Technology

Bill was practically illiterate when it came to computers. But he jumped into a crash learning mode more ambitious than anything he'd attempted since mastering dental technology. Bill quickly discovered that he wasn't alone in his ignorance. Even self-styled Internet "experts" were often just a few steps ahead of him on the learning curve.

"The field is so new," says Bill, "that there are a lot of entrepreneurs out there trying to jump on the bandwagon as so-called Internet service providers when they barely understand the technology themselves."

Provider Problems

Bill got his daughter to handle a lot of the programming and to help design the Web pages. But he still needed professional providers to store those pages on a Web server—a computer that gives access to the Internet. That's where Bill ran into trouble.

"A lot of times, you would tell them what you want and they would say, 'Okay, we can do that,' and then for weeks or months they would just make excuses why they weren't doing it. Often, the problem was they just didn't have the professional expertise to manage a Web server.

"In some cases, we found that our pages were down more than they were up. The information we put together was not accessible to anybody because they were having this technical problem or that technical problem. We went through four different providers before we found one that could handle the job, and we lost about nine months."

People Power

The key to Bill's vision was service—helping prospects learn all they needed to know about Oxyfresh, without any sales pressure, and helping individual Oxyfresh distributors gain access to interested prospects, with little or no time investment on their part. For a $1,000 fee, Bill offered to help each co-op member create a home page and to link that home page to the Oxyfresh corporate Web site.

Thus, a prospect surfing the Web for network marketing opportunities might wander onto the Oxyfresh home page, where he could browse through a product catalog, order items, peruse information about the company, or even sign up as a distributor via e-mail. If the prospect was looking for a sponsor, he could view a comprehensive list of co-op members, broken down by geographic location.

"Say you're in Kansas," Bill explains. "On our Web site, you could find several distributors in your area. You'd be able to read through their personal stories and find a story of someone you felt you could connect to. You could say, 'Hey, this person is a lot like me and is doing this business and is successful, so maybe I can do it too.' That's what I've always felt is the power in this company. It's the personal stories of people."

High Tech, High Touch

Once he had his own personal home page posted, Bill was surprised at the emotional impact it often had on prospects.

"What I have found is that after people have read my story on the Web site, it's very easy to converse with them on the phone, because now they know who I am, and that trust is already established. It's as if I'm a long-lost buddy. I don't even know them, but they know me. It makes prospecting very very easy."

A Leader

As Oxyfresh's resident Webmaster, Bill found himself playing a new role as leader and teacher—a job that fit him like a glove. As applications for co-op membership poured in, it quickly became evident that most of the applicants had little or no knowledge of computers.

"We'd end up spending a lot of time training them technically on how to use their computer, how to access their Web pages, how to cut and paste, and how to do e-mail," says Bill.

In an eerie reminder of his own past sessions with frustrated sponsors, Bill now found himself whipping procrastinators and foot-draggers into shape. Bill had banged out his own life story quickly and posted it right away. The important thing was to get it online, he thought. There'd be plenty of time later for editing and fine-tuning. But other co-op members froze like deer in the headlights. Overwhelmed at the thought of displaying their life stories for millions to see, they would invent one excuse after another to delay submitting their final drafts.

"One guy said he rewrote his story ten times before he ever submitted it to us," says Bill. "I never anticipated that that would happen."

Prospecting by Contest

One of Bill's key innovations was an online contest designed to draw traffic to the site and harvest leads. Through a monthly drawing, he offered to give away $100 worth of Oxyfresh products. Each applicant clicks "yes" or "no" in response to three questions:

- Would you be interested in subscribing to our monthly newsletter?
- Would you be interested in building a part-time or full-time home-based business and seeing if that would work for you?
- Would you like to learn how to leverage yourself to have personal and financial freedom?

Prospects are also asked to rate themselves on a scale of 1 to 10, with 1 being "not at this time" and 10 being "extremely interested." Based on their answers, prospects are prioritized according to three different categories—hot, warm, or cold—and automatically distributed to co-op members via e-mail "auto-responder."

Kaizen

So absorbed did he become in his technical tasks that Bill was taken completely by surprise when he suddenly discovered that he had become a network marketing celebrity. In September 1995, the leading trade publication, *Upline,* ran a profile of Bill and his remarkable Web site. Immediately, Bill's phone started ringing off the hook. Distributors from other companies offered Bill top dollar to put up similar Web sites for them. But Bill turned them down.

"I felt that was a conflict of interest for me," Bill explains. "Besides, it takes all my time just creating the Oxyfresh site."

Bill feels he's in a "horse race" now with other MLM companies jumping on the Internet bandwagon. To stay ahead, he practices *kaizen*—the Japanese philosophy of continual, incremental improvement.

"These other companies on the Internet are constantly updating their sites," says Bill. "So we've got to do the same, if we want to stay ahead of the game."

Cosmic Justice

Today, Bill still operates a dental lab in his home and leases out another lab in Salt Lake City. He takes as much pride in his dental work as he ever did. But at last Bill has found a way to serve and contribute in his Oxyfresh business with the same diligence and effectiveness with which he grinds dental prostheses.

In the first six months of 1996 alone, Bill's Web site (http://oxyfresh.com) experienced over 160,000 hits and generated nearly 10,000 leads for co-op members. For this invaluable service to his fellow distributors, Bill has already reaped some personal rewards. For one thing, the Web site has begun generating some promising leads for Bill's own downline, offering him the long-sought opportunity for instigating massive action with minimal time investment. And, in a remarkable turn of the cosmic wheel, Bill recently found himself the recipient of a wholly unexpected—but remarkably appropriate—bonus.

Thanks to his Oxyfresh earnings, Bill was able to pay cash for a time-share condo in Park City, Utah. Because the condo was still under construction, buyers were offered an incentive of a free round-trip ticket for two to anywhere in the world, plus accommodations. It shouldn't take readers too many guesses to figure out what vacation destination Bill selected. In April 1996, he and Susan finally set off on their dream trip to New Zealand and Australia. You can bet that Bill made sure to pack his fly-fishing tackle.

Chapter 9

AUTO-TRAINING

Vern Steyer was furious. When he answered the ad for a business opportunity in the local paper, the last thing he was looking for was a network marketing company. Vern would never have shown up for the meeting had he known it was MLM. Over the years, Vern had had more than his fill of network marketing. In his first company, he had struggled for years, earning only a pittance. His second company had been shut down by the Florida state attorney general's office as a pyramid scam. That's when Vern decided to steer clear of the industry altogether. Yet, here he was, suckered once more into attending an MLM opportunity meeting!

"I was disgusted at myself," Vern recalls. "While the speaker was talking, I mentally reached over to the volume dial and turned it way down low. If it hadn't been pouring down rain that night, I probably would have got up and left."

The Single Greatest Burden

A schoolteacher by profession, Vern seemed ill-suited for the MLM life. The high-intensity prospecting and training that successful network marketers were required to do during the Wave-Two era was not only unpleasant to Vern but downright dangerous. His delicate heart condition made it imperative that Vern take it easy and avoid pressure.

As he sat in that meeting wallowing in disgust, Vern had no idea that he was about to encounter a new type of network marketing, one that would remove many of the pressures he'd felt in past opportunities. More and more, cutting-edge MLM firms have come to recognize that training your downline is the single greatest burden on the individual distributor. You can recruit 500 people a month, but if you can't train them to work the business, they won't add a penny to your cash flow. The demands of training thus create a double burden on network marketers like Vern, who would prefer to focus more effort on growing their organizations.

The Total Training Environment

Many companies have responded by investing in auto-training technology—videotapes, audiotapes, teleconferences, and satellite TV broadcasts that walk new distributors through the basics. But if the business itself is overly difficult to learn, such flashy solutions are little better than gimmickry. The most expensive video in the world will not help a distributor to understand a comp plan that has been designed with Byzantine complexity. The slickest satellite broadcast will never help distributors move a product line that is overpriced for the market, isn't consumable, or is too technical to explain without putting your potential customers to sleep.

For that reason, Wave-Three companies today have begun to focus on creating total business environments in which the procedures are so simple, recruits practically train themselves. The latest wave of auto-training still uses videos, satellite broadcasts, and the like, but combines these tools with comp plans, product lines, and selling procedures so streamlined that most recruits can master them without any special instruction. All they have to do is watch you and imitate what you do.

As Vern Steyer growled and grumbled through that opportunity meeting, he had no idea that he was about to enter the magical world of the Wave-Three training environment—an experience that not only would change his opinion of MLM, but would profoundly enhance the quality of his life.

A Different Sales Pitch

Through most of the presentation, Vern sulked and stewed. He heard very little of it. But toward the end, the presenter—a man named Al Thomas—said something that made Vern's ears prick up.

"Some of you here tonight have had some experience in network marketing," said Al.

Yeah, Vern grumped silently, *I've had some experience in that, and I could probably teach you a thing or two about it, young fellow.*

"As a matter of fact," Al continued, "some of you may have had some pretty good success in network marketing and then it all sort of fell apart, because people stopped selling the product, the volume went down, and so did your income."

Despite himself, Vern couldn't help sitting up in his seat. *That's exactly one hundred percent correct,* he thought. Al Thomas was describing the precise experience Vern had undergone in his first MLM business. Without even realizing it, Vern was suddenly hanging on Al's every word.

"To be honest with you," Al continued, "if you become an Excel representative, there are some people out there who are going to lose the vision. They're going to give up. They're going to quit. But . . ." Here, Al's gaze swept the room, seeming to pierce into every soul, "do you think that, in the process of quitting, *they're going to call every one of their customers and tell them to go back to AT&T so that they can spend more money on their long-distance charges?"*

Vern was stunned. It hit him like a lightning bolt. Of course they wouldn't do that! If you were selling long-distance phone service, whatever customers you had would stay in the system, no matter how many people dropped out of your downline. As long as they saved money on their long-distance calls, why would they leave?

Maybe there really is something different about this opportunity, Vern thought. Although he had sworn off network marketing years ago, Vern had to admit that there were still times when he found himself pondering what might have been. In his heart, some small, lonely ember of faith and hope still burned. Now, as he donned his coat, grabbed his umbrella, and slumped out into the rain, Vern could feel that spark beginning to kindle in his chest for the first time in years.

AN UNTOLD STORY

In 1987, two upstart companies called U.S. Sprint and MCI stole away 15 percent of AT&T's long-distance market share. The corporate world was astounded. But press reports failed to explain exactly how the feat was accomplished. Only a handful of business visionaries did enough homework to learn that network marketing had been the key. Both MCI and U.S. Sprint had made heavy use of third-party MLM sales forces.

One of these visionaries was a Texas oil man named Kenny Troutt. Inspired by U.S. Sprint's MLM coup, Troutt and his partner, Steve Smith, founded Dallas-based Excel Telecommunications—a company that sold long-distance service solely through network marketing.

This is the company that Vern Steyer was looking at on that rainy night in January 1993. His timing could not have been more perfect. In the following two years, Excel grew over 300 percent and, by year-end 1995, it had reached over half a billion dollars in sales.

A Unique Training System

Excel had far more going for it than just the right product at the right time. Many MLMs selling long-distance phone service had come and gone, enjoying a single dramatic spike in growth only to wither away in the next few months. But Excel had staying power. What drove Excel was not so much its cheap long-distance rates but a carefully crafted business environment that cut down on training time and actually *paid* distributors for what little training they had to do. This potent combination of Wave-Three support systems allowed almost anyone to effectively manage an extensive downline.

Train by Example

"How you do your recruiting is 75 percent of your training," says Colli Butler of FreeLife. "The way you bring your recruits into the business is the same way they'll bring others into the business."

It sounds easy. But, in the Wave-Two era, how you did your recruiting was not necessarily something you *wanted* your recruits to imitate. With few standard procedures to guide them, Wave-Two recruiters often expended massive time and effort to attain paltry results. If your downline imitated recruiting methods like those, they would likely get discouraged and quit.

The "75 percent" principle works only when your business system is both effective and easy to duplicate.

Maximize *duplicatability* in every aspect of your operations, from prospecting to product fulfillment, and training will take care of itself. Your primary job as a leader will then be to stay out of the way and resist the temptation to complicate things.

THE TRAINING BARRIER

Right about the time that Vern Steyer was sitting in on that meeting in Sacramento, California, another couple in a nearby town was also taking a look at Excel. Michael and Barbara Lammons were polar opposites to Vern in temperament and background. Vern was a retired schoolteacher looking for part-time income. The Lammons were hard-driving entrepreneurs looking to start a successful business. But both had been cheated of their dreams when they ran smack up against the Training Barrier.

After ten years of owning and running two health clubs, Michael and Barbara Lammons had decided that they never again wanted to train or supervise another employee. No amount of training seemed capable of instilling a work ethic, a sense of responsibility, or even basic common sense into most of the college kids and other minimum-wage workers who staffed their clubs. The moment the Lammons' backs were turned, things went haywire.

"You could never really leave," says Barbara. "Every time we left town, some disaster happened, like when one of our employees turned off the wrong breaker switch and set off the fire alarm."

The Greatest Luxury

Michael and Barbara were caught in the employer trap. The bigger their business grew, the more employees they had to hire and train. Yet, instead of relieving them of work, their growing staff only added to their burden.

"We worked seven days a week," says Barbara. "And long hours. My husband was up at 4 A.M. everyday. The club opened at 5 A.M., and he would be down there.

"What bothered me most is that we couldn't even stop to rest. No matter how many employees we hired, we could never rely on them to just take over for us. My dream was that one day I'd be able to just go to bed at night and know that I did not have to get up in the morning, that it was a matter of choice. That would have been the greatest luxury I could imagine."

The MLM Option

Despite all their hard work at the health clubs, the Lammons had never succeeded in making real money. After ten years, they had yet to buy health insurance or put away money for retirement. That's when the Lammons decided they'd had enough. They sold the clubs and started looking around for other options.

While Michael made some halfhearted stabs at selling insurance, Barbara scanned the classifieds. One ad caught her eye. It said: "Own your own business. Part-time. Full-time. Telecommunications industry." When she called the number, however, Barbara was dismayed to learn that the business involved network marketing.

"We always felt that network marketing was for people who couldn't get a real job," she admits.

Still, times were tough. Barbara no longer felt she had the luxury of being so choosy. So she dragged Michael to an opportunity meeting for Excel. Barbara's efforts seemed in vain. Michael glowered angrily throughout the entire meeting. Afterward, he flatly declared that there was no money to be made in this business and he wasn't going to work it.

Word-of-Mouth Marketing

"I knew I couldn't do this without my husband's help," says Barbara. "The two of us would have to work as a team."

Nevertheless, Barbara went alone to her first Excel training class. Despite her husband's nay-saying, she saw many strengths in the concept.

"From marketing our health clubs, I knew how advertising-blind the public is," says Barbara. "All the money that we spent on TV and newspaper ads—we might as well have gone to Las Vegas and just gambled it away. If you're with a big company that can invest millions, then advertising works. But for a small business owner, it's always a gamble. I knew that the best promotions we ever ran at the health club were the in-house promotions where we encouraged members to bring in a friend. So I understood the power of word-of-mouth marketing."

Barbara went ahead and signed up her husband. She knew he wouldn't be pleased. But after all the bum deals Michael had roped them into over the years (like the mini-mart, where they'd dumped $300,000), Barbara also knew he wouldn't have the nerve to complain too loudly.

Auto-Motivation

Without realizing it, Barbara had already begun her husband's training regimen. She signed him on as a customer, a sales representative, and an "area coordinator"—Excel's term for an entry-level trainer. The whole package had cost $525, including $130 to register as a distributor, get a starter kit, and subscribe to the company newsletter, and $395 to become a trainer, which included all necessary presentation materials.

Michael may not have been happy about being an Excel distributor. But at least he started out with a clear goal: to make back the money Barbara had already spent.

"His number one goal," says Barbara, "was to get back the $525, by sponsoring five people as representatives. By the time he accomplished that, he was hooked."

The Know-Nothing Approach

Barbara had one problem. She couldn't explain to her husband how the marketing plan worked. Nor could she explain exactly how Excel would help people save money on their long-distance bills. All of that had been explained during the training she took. But it had gone in one ear and out the other. If Barbara didn't understand it herself and couldn't explain it to her husband, how were they going to be able to sell it to customers and prospects?

That's when Barbara began to grasp the utter simplicity of the business. In fact, she didn't need to know all these facts and figures. If she did, they would likely only bore and confuse her prospects as much as they had confused her in the training session. The one thing that stuck in Barbara's mind were the words her sponsor had said during that first business presentation:

"Just try it for one month. At the end of the month, compare your new long-distance bill with your old one. If you didn't save money with Excel, then fine, don't use it. But if you *did* save money, don't you think you'd like to stay on as an Excel customer? And don't you think you could find a lot of other people who would like to do the same?"

That was about the easiest sales pitch you could imagine, thought Barbara. It was easy to remember and easy to use. What's more, as Michael and Barbara were about to find out, it really worked. It worked, first of all, for the Lammons themselves. During their first month as Excel customers, they immediately saved money.

"Both of our children lived on opposite ends of the state," says Barbara, "so every call to them was long distance. Our phone bill was cut significantly by being on the service. So that gave us a lot of confidence in selling it to others."

Don't Argue

Barbara and Michael quickly discovered that it was pointless to argue with people. Once you had asked them to try the service, they either would or they wouldn't. There was nothing else to discuss.

"You'll know it in the first 30 seconds," says Barbara.

Recruiting business builders was a little more involved, but not much. Mike and Barbara were urged to use the "second-look principle." After pitching prospects on the business, you encouraged them to go home and think about it.

"Then you would contact them later to see if they wanted to do it," says Barbara. "You want to give them time to really look at the business, see it for what it is and how it would fit into their life. If they're not interested after thinking about it for a couple of days, it's probably not right for them, and they're not the people you want anyway."

No Rush

Business builders in Excel are encouraged to start out by gathering 20 customers. However, there is no penalty for failing to meet that goal in a given time period. Distributors work at their own pace.

"We chose to work fast," says Barbara, "because we wanted to build a business. But we weren't obliged to, in any way."

Others, less ambitious than the Lammons, have managed to build Excel businesses at a more leisurely pace. Vern Steyer, for example, took things easy. He started out at the same time as the Lammons. But Vern had no interest in pursuing the business full-time. In fact, after his third month, Vern took his wife on a five-and-a-half-week vacation. It wasn't until Vern's fifth month in the business that he finally acquired his first 20 customers, and it took him a full two years to reach executive director, the highest commission level in the company.

A Second Income

Despite his slow pace, Vern's income climbed briskly. That's because, in Excel, distributors are paid not only commissions on sales but also a separate fee for training their recruits.

As an area coordinator—the lowest level of trainer in Excel—you are paid $40 for each new representative you train. The trainings are held once a week and take about two hours. All you do is show the training videos and answer questions. When you attain the rank of regional training director, you are qualified to train new area coordinators, for which you are paid $80 per trainee and $100 each when you become a national training director—a position Vern Steyer now holds.

"In my past MLM businesses," says Vern, "I would spend my entire Saturday doing workshops and training people. The only compensation I could hope for was the possibility that I might move a bit more volume of product as a result of training those people. Now, for the first time, I feel that I'm being properly compensated for that effort."

Meetingless Meetings

Because they have set higher goals than most, Michael and Barbara Lammons choose to spend a lot of time on the road, working with their downline around the country. Nevertheless, wherever they go, the Excel training system goes with them, streamlining their tasks and making their job easier. Meetings are a cinch, because they are so tightly packaged and formatted.

"It's a quick presentation, because it's scripted," says Barbara. "You follow the Excel script and do just what it says, and it lasts about 20 minutes."

Afterward, the Lammons ask the guests to meet with the person who brought them, to have their questions answered.

"Anyone is welcome to bring their questions directly to us, of course," says Barbara, "but it's not necessary. Any trained rep in the room should be able to answer any question. In this business, once you've been trained, you're trained. Excel has really taken the burden off of having to educate a representative a whole lot. There just isn't a whole lot to know."

Anyone Can Do It

On one occasion, a lady with tattoos all over her body and loads of earrings jangling from each ear showed up at a training. Michael took her aside and suggested, as tactfully as he could, that her sales might improve if she polished up her image.

"I can do this business just as well as you," the woman countered. "All my friends have phones and my friends will not come and listen to someone like you. But they'll listen to me. I can reach a whole group of people that you never could."

And she was right. The woman quickly built up a group and became a regional director. Michael was chastened by the experience. Even he had underestimated the duplicatability of the Excel system.

The Ultimate Vending Machine Route

Back in the days when he was slaving away as a public school teacher, Vern Steyer used to daydream about owning vending machines. He imagined placing machines in good locations all over town and then sitting back and just waiting for people to fill those machines with dimes and quarters. Recently, as Vern was driving behind a man in a little pickup loaded with vending machines, Vern was reminded of his old dream. It dawned on him that his Excel business has given him something even better.

"I realized that I now have the ultimate vending machine route," says Vern. "I have the equivalent of all of those machines out there. But I didn't have to buy them and I didn't have to go out and place them in their locations."

Vern now has over 700 distributors in his seven-level pay range and over 5,400 phone customers. Anytime one of those 4,500 customers picks up the phone to make a long-distance call, Vern makes money. He never has to handle or stockpile any product.

"Pushing the product is what really turns a lot of people off in network marketing," says Vern. "You've got to forever be pushing that product, and it gets a little old after a while. I don't care how good that product is. You get real weary of it. But, in my Excel business, I don't have to remind any of my customers to make long-distance phone calls. It's an unconscious buying decision."

A Part-Time Job

As a retiree, Vern has little interest in working hard. And he doesn't have to. He typically spends three nights a week in meetings and one night a week training. The rest of the week he meets with people over lunch or coffee to pitch them on the business.

"I have a sufficient number of personal customers now," says Vern, "so that I never have to personally gather another customer the rest of my life. All of my attention can be devoted to recruiting representatives and helping them get started and making them successful."

An Enviable Existence

Not long ago, Vern went to an accountant to get his taxes done. During their meeting, the accountant's partner stuck his head in the door and greeted Vern.

"You making any money yet at this phone thing?" the man asked.

"Well, it's not exactly what I'd like to be making," said Vern. "But I'm doing okay."

Vern then showed the man his 1099 form. As a result, he sponsored both accountants into the business.

A System for the Future

Barbara Lammons still works hard. But, nowadays, when she gets up in the morning, she does it by choice. The Lammons have long since become millionaires through their Excel business. Their monthly bonus checks average in the low six figures. The days when they had to endure the headaches and frustrations of being "the boss" seem like a distant memory now. Unlike the feckless employees at their old health clubs, the 26,000 distributors in the Lammons' personal organization can be relied upon to keep doing their jobs even when the boss isn't looking. That's not because they're better people. It's because they work in a better system.

"Excel has taught me an entirely new world of business," says Barbara, "which I believe is the way of the future. There's never been an opportunity as user-friendly as this."

Fifty years ago, the pioneers of network marketing promised the world a business opportunity at which virtually anyone could succeed. The industry has a long way to go before it fulfills that promise to the letter. But the advent of auto-training systems such as those Vern Steyer and the Lammons have exploited so successfully has surely brought that day much closer than it has ever been before.

Chapter 10

WAVE-THREE LEADERSHIP

K ate Gill-Grossi was mortified. Not only had she failed
to win over her prospect, but Kate had the awful feeling that she had made a fool of herself in the process.
Her prospect was a friend and colleague from Kate's corporate past, a high-level consultant. He had listened respect-
fully enough to her sales pitch. But, again and again, the
man kept interrupting with the same question.

"I understand the concept," he said. "It's the nuts and
bolts I don't get. You still haven't explained to me how you
really make money in this business."

Each time he said it, his words stabbed at Kate like a
knife. The man was right. Her explanation of the compensation plan was vague and superficial. Kate too had come
from the corporate world. Before entering network marketing, she had been, at various times, a consultant, a
company vice president, and a partner in her own company. Kate understood the high standards expected of a
corporate sales presentation. And she was acutely aware
that her presentation today was not meeting them.

Unfortunately, there was nothing Kate could do
about that. She couldn't explain the comp plan because
she herself did not understand it. Bravely, she struggled
on, repeating by rote the slogans and catchphrases she'd
heard from her sponsor. But even as they poured from her
mouth, Kate realized how absurd and evasive they
sounded. She wasn't at all surprised when the man finally cut her short and said he wasn't interested.

"I didn't want to ruin our friendship, so I backed off," Kate recalls. "But I felt awful. And that sort of thing happened to me time and time again through my first six months in the business."

The Cutting Edge

Kate didn't realize it, but she had arrived at the cutting edge of the Wave-Three revolution. And she herself was the knife. As a leader, Kate really had only one acceptable option when faced with a problem—to solve it. In solving this particular problem, she not only made her own job easier, but spurred the industry toward a new level of sophistication.

From the inception of network marketing, the industry's evolution has been driven by leaders like Kate Gill-Grossi. Frustrated by the clumsy methods of Wave-Two MLM companies, millions of rank-and-file distributors have fled the industry in despair. But those with a taste and talent for leadership have responded to the challenge in a different way.

With resourcefulness, energy, and grim determination, they have forged ahead, creating unique solutions to the problems they encountered. As they build their downlines, these leaders revolutionize prospecting techniques, rewrite compensation plans, and train whole new generations in the Wave Three Way.

The Grass Roots

Even today, while more and more companies are adopting Wave-Three standards at the corporate level, the cutting edge of innovation remains solidly at the grass roots, among the upline leaders. A single company might have two or more different legs in its downline, each one reflecting business philosophies that span the wide gap between

Wave-Two and Wave-Three methodologies. The corporate culture of any given leg in a company depends heavily on the character of the leader at the top. Before joining any company, wise network marketers will carefully scrutinize the upline leaders, choosing only those legs of an MLM organization that seem committed to change.

Corporate Burnout

After 15 years of climbing the corporate ladder, Kate Gill-Grossi was burnt out. She made $180,000 per year in salary and stock options as vice president of an economic consulting firm in the San Francisco Bay area. But she paid for it with her freedom.

"I had two small children at home, ages two and three, who were being raised by a full-time nanny," says Kate, "I wanted to do something that would allow me more flexibility to spend time with my family."

When Kate answered a blind ad for an "area sales manager," she was furious to find herself, 24 hours later, sitting in a network marketing presentation for a company that sold water purifiers. Nevertheless, her curiosity piqued, Kate stayed and listened to the speaker.

"During the course of that meeting," she says, "it really hit me what a great way this was to make a living, having a home-based business."

Kate resolved to make a thorough study of the industry. In 1989, convinced that there was real opportunity in network marketing, she joined the company.

The Learning Curve

It wasn't long before Kate ran smack into the problem that all MLM neophytes encounter sooner or later: the learning curve. Her corporate background proved to be of little help to her in this new arena. For the first six months in the business, Kate floundered helplessly.

"The training that you get with network marketing tends to be very motivational," says Kate. "It keeps you in the business, but it doesn't show you how to do the business."

Kate went to training after training, listening to speakers talk about self-discipline, persistence, and positive attitude. The more of these speeches she heard, the more irritated she became.

"I was already successful in the corporate world," she says. "I didn't need to be self-empowered. What I needed was to learn how the business worked. I would leave each training furious because I hadn't learned anything useful."

Money, Not Position

Kate knew she could run circles around most of the people she saw up on that stage. But first, she would have to learn the business. And, because she had no teacher, Kate resolved that she would teach herself.

She had noticed that many distributors urged their recruits to work toward higher *positions* in the company—honorary titles that granted special status and higher commissions. The problem was that you could attain these positions simply by plugging recruits into certain positions in your downline and buying a certain amount of inventory each month. You didn't have to sell a thing. The result was a lot of people running around with big positions but no earnings. That observation gave Kate her first clue to MLM success. *Forget position,* Kate told herself. *Concentrate on sales volume.*

Drive Your Paycheck

But how much sales volume would she really need in order to attain her goals? It was a simple question, but Kate could find no answers from her fellow distributors. Nobody seemed to understand the comp plan well enough to calculate exactly how much sales volume you would need to earn a given amount of monthly commission! Most of them just worked blindly away, thanking God whenever the company computer spit out a check for them.

For a former vice president like Kate, that was no way to run a railroad. She sat down one day and did what none of her fellow distributors had yet bothered to do—she studied the compensation plan until she knew it cold.

"I figured out exactly, on a daily basis, how many people I'd have to recruit and how much sales volume each one would have to do, in order for me to make, say, $10,000 per month," she says.

Brick by Brick

Kate then called a meeting of her top five distributors and announced to them her goal of generating $100,000 in sales volume that month. Each of the five leaders in Kate's group was assigned to move $20,000.

"We went out and massively recruited," says Kate. "I held each group leader accountable for doing $1,000 personally, and then finding 19 other people who would do $1,000 each. We built it brick by brick, through a lot of people each doing a little bit."

The Structure-Building Method

Kate had taken the first step in creating her "structural" method of downline building. As the weeks progressed, she honed down her technique to six simple steps:

1. *Set your target volume.* Determine, according to your company's compensation plan, how much sales volume your organization must move each

month in order for you to generate the monthly income you desire.

2. *Break down the volume to micronumbers.* Divide up the target sales volume by 100. You now have 100 small units (or micronumbers) that 100 individuals can easily achieve.

3. *Do structure calls.* Call up the top business builders in your downline. Ask them what their goals are, how much time they are spending on the business, how many good prospects they have in the pipeline. In general, you'll find that only two out of twelve are really active. Cross out the rest. You now have two active business builders (or an equivalent proportion) that you can count on. Work from there.

4. *Set recruiting goals.* Subtract the number of active distributors you have from the number of distributors you *need* (Kate advises shooting for 100). If you have only two active distributors, that means you need 98 more. Now divide 98 by your two distributors, to get 49. That means that each of your distributors must recruit 49 people (however, see the next step).

5. *Set microrecruiting goals.* Much as you did for the sales volume, assign each of your active distributors a small, doable recruiting goal. You can't expect your two distributors to recruit 49 people apiece. That's way too many for one month. But if each of your two distributors recruits seven people who recruit seven apiece, they will meet their goal. Of course, in real life, some of your distributors will be more capable than others. You may want to skew the responsibilities accordingly, assigning higher goals to some people and lower goals to others, making sure the total balances out.

6. *Do a leadership call.* Call up your active distributors and assign them their microsales and microrecruiting goals. Then get to work!

Build Proper Structure

Every compensation plan has its own peculiar structure that must be taken into account when projecting earnings. In many plans, for example, distributors who are recruited on different levels of your organization will contribute different percentages of commission. Kate took these differences into account when assigning microsales and microrecruiting goals. In working with new recruits, she would sit down and draw up an organizational chart that showed how to meet that recruit's goals *within the commission structure* of her company's particular plan.

Unfortunately, there is no shortcut to understanding comp plans. The subject could easily fill another book. If your company does not provide specific training on this subject (and most don't), it is your responsibility as a Wave-Three leader to do the homework for your downline, as Kate Gill-Grossi did.

A Ripple Effect

After instituting her micronumbers approach, Kate experienced what she calls a "ripple effect" (what we know as the Butterfly Effect).

"It was a revelation," she says. "By figuring this thing out, I became immediately duplicatable, because it was something that I could teach that made sense, that other people could grasp. It made an enormous difference in my business. Enormous."

In three months, Kate leaped from $12,000 per month in sales to $100,000. When she finally left that company 18 months later, she was personally earning about $10,000 per month.

The Bigger the Paycheck, the Stronger the Glue

Today, Kate is a frontline leader for The Peoples Network (TPN) along with her partner, Darren Hardy. Using her structure-building approach, Kate helps each new recruit build an organization designed to produce the precise level of income they require.

"My goal is to help people achieve the biggest paycheck possible," Kate explains, "because that's what holds an organization together. The bigger the paycheck, the stronger the glue."

When Kate gets her recruits started, she helps them determine a realistic goal for their first two paychecks. Then she walks them through the process of calculating exactly how many people they need to prospect, how many will probably say no, how many business briefings they will have to have, and how many hours they need to spend in order to have x number of people in the pipeline by the end of the month.

"They leave the training with an exact blueprint for achieving their goals," says Kate.

She Did It Her Way

In a Fortune 500 company, Kate's nuts and bolts approach to building sales volume would be taken for granted. Unfortunately, it is still considered exceptional among network marketers.

"I do my training completely differently from anyone I've ever met," says Kate. "People come to my trainings and say, 'You're teaching me stuff that I've never heard, and I've been in the industry for three years.' Even within

TPN, there are two different groups. Between our group and the other group, there's a totally different training, a totally different concept. It's like night and day."

Don't Motivate—Empower!

According to Kate Gill-Grossi, the best way to motivate people is to empower them with practical knowledge. Her structure-building approach is a prototype for the future. It is, in fact, the Wave Three Way. As the Wave-Three Revolution progresses, we can expect to see a lot more training that follows Kate's model.

"We are attracting a much higher caliber of person in the industry now," says Kate. "You have got to be able to put together a business plan that makes sense to a sophisticated person."

THE EVOLVING COMP PLAN

Kate Gill-Grossi shows distributors how to get the most from their existing comp plans. Other leaders are working on the "supply" end of the Wave Three Way—helping companies design better plans in the first place.

Over 17 years, Len Clements worked seven different MLM companies. Like most network marketers, Len took a lot of hard knocks. Unlike most, he put these lessons to work in developing a revolutionary new concept of the business, described in Len's best-selling book, *Inside Network Marketing,* previously published as *Beyond the Veil.*

Len noticed that many people, when shopping for an MLM company, tend to ask the wrong questions, such as, "How much does the company pay out?"

"People think if a company claims a 72 percent payout, it must be a well-paying plan," says Len. "But there's usually a vast difference between the theoretic maximum payout and the actual payout."

Hidden Breakage

The problem, according to Len, is *breakage:* sales volume that comes into your organization but for which you receive no commission due to special provisions in your compensation plan.

According to Len, few MLM companies could survive if they paid out more than 50 cents on every sales dollar to their distributors. Yet, companies routinely claim that they pay more, in order to gain a competitive edge. After offering impossible payouts, companies then protect themselves from bankruptcy by building breakage into the plan—using sly rules that subtly siphon off your actual earnings—so that the distributor force never *really* receives more than 50 percent of total revenues—and usually receives considerably less.

Volume, Not Payout

A compulsive focus on payout also ignores a more fundamental issue in a company's success—sales volume.

"Seventy-five percent of zero is still zero," Len comments. "A company with a great payout but poor sales is not as good an opportunity as a company with a low payout but doing a large volume of sales."

In their efforts to finance higher and higher payouts, companies must continually jack up the prices of products, which is why so many network marketers are going around trying to peddle $25 bottles of shampoo. Such overpricing drives away customers and lowers sales volume, creating an inverse relationship between payout and actual earnings.

A Big Fish Without a Pond

Through years of experience and study, Len established himself as an industry expert, a nationally known trainer, and an all-around "big fish." His monthly newsletter *Market-Wave* (now called *Profit Now*) reviews and evaluates MLM opportunities and comp plans. It has become to network marketing what *Publishers Weekly* is to the book business. Yet, despite Len's apparent success, until recently he never managed to find a network marketing company to call home.

Meeting of the Minds

Then, one day in November 1993, Len attended a two-day marketing and promotion workshop with MLM trainer Tom Schreiter. During the seminar, he had what would prove to be a fateful dinner with three industry colleagues.

"It happened that we were all between companies," says Len, "or just getting ready to leave a company."

The four men traded MLM war stories until late in the evening. All turned out to have drawn similar conclusions about the industry.

"We were disgusted with the level of training and support," says Len. "We all wondered why the industry couldn't do a better job of supporting distributors."

Len suggested, half-jokingly, that he and his three dinner companions create an organization themselves that would offer such support. They could form a partnership, find a promising MLM company, and join it as a group, supplying their downline with the best training and support possible.

An All-Star Team

To Len's surprise, his dinner companions loved the idea. In the days and weeks ahead, through a number of telephone conference calls, they laid the groundwork for what would become a unique phenomenon in the annals of MLM—the FreeStyles Group.

One of the FreeStylers was Gary Carson. He brought to the table all of his facilities and staff at FirstNet—a company offering third-party support services to the MLM industry, including graphic art, design services, and telecommunications. Carson's participation enabled the FreeStyles Group to offer its distributors state-of-the-art voice-mail and fax-on-demand service, marketing materials, and Web site design and other Internet support.

FreeStyler Corey Augenstein was a well-respected industry "watch-dog," a newsletter publisher known for his objectivity and Ralph Nader–like advocacy of distributor rights. Corey had never joined an MLM company before. His presence on the team would amount to a *Good Housekeeping* seal ensuring high ethical standards.

The final FreeStyler was Phil Longenecker, publisher of the magazine *Cutting Edge Opportunities*. He brought to the table considerable expertise in the areas of advertising, marketing, and lead generation.

Behind the Growth Curve

The partners selected a likely looking startup company and began building a downline. In the first five months, they built an organization of 2,600 people. Then the trouble started.

"The company got behind the growth curve," says Len.

Overfast growth is the second most common cause of MLM failures after undercapitalization (otherwise known as not having enough cash in the bank). When a company's sales outgrow its infrastructure and management capacity, things can fall apart quickly.

"It's like letting go of the reins of a wild horse," says Len. "All of a sudden, distributors find themselves back-ordering products or getting their checks late or not at all. When you call company headquarters to find out what's up, you get a lot of long waits and busy signals. It's a real mess."

Changing a Tire at 50 Miles an Hour

Before long, according to Len, the company began showing all the classic symptoms of what are euphemistically termed "growing pains."

At one point, the company began changing its comp plan every month, leaving distributors in a chronic state of confusion. Then it upgraded its computer system in the midst of a heavy growth cycle.

"That's the worst time to do it," says Len. "It's like changing a tire at 50 miles an hour. Anytime you upgrade computer systems, add more phone lines, or move to a larger facility, you create havoc for the distributors. Those things should be done *before* the rapid growth kicks in. But most companies don't have the foresight or the capital to do it that way."

Management Stability

As distributors began fleeing the company in droves, Len and his fellow FreeStylers had to face the fact that they'd backed the wrong horse. In assessing companies, they had failed to consider one key criterion: management stability. That's the ability of a company's managers to keep an even keel through downturns and upturns alike.

"It's easy to check a company's finances," says Len. "It's easy to check out its product line and evaluate its comp plan. But management stability is much harder to judge. There's almost no way to do it, except to join the company and see what happens when the growth hits."

In Search of the Triple-A Company

Once again, the FreeStylers set out in search of the perfect opportunity. For a solid month, they reviewed one company after another. Although they found many good companies, none could meet the exceptionally high standards they had set.

"Every company, no matter how good it looked in the beginning, turned out to have some serious flaw," says Len. "We could find companies, say, with two A's and a C—great comp plan, great company, lousy product. Or great product, great company, lousy comp plan. But forget about three A's. We would have settled for two A's and a B, but we couldn't even find that."

A Lucky Break

The FreeStylers had just about decided to settle on a considerably less than perfect company, when Len had a lucky break. A man named Jim Song called to inquire about putting an ad in Len's newsletter *MarketWave*. Jim and his wife Adi had a new company called Longevity Network, which offered a line of health and nutrition products. At Len's request, Jim sent a pack of samples.

"The next day, he overnighted to me what they call a career pack," says Len, "which included one of every product in the line, along with all the literature. It was like Christmas morning here opening up this box, with all these products spilling out all over my floor. I was just in awe of the product line and the packaging."

Transfer Sale

Equally impressive to Len were the low retail prices. Many MLM companies claim to offer distributors an easy "transfer" sale. In other words, they claim that their product simply replaces some common, consumable item that people are going to buy anyway, such as shampoo. Theoretically, it should be easier to sell such an item, because your potential customers have already included it in their weekly budgets.

Unfortunately, the inflated prices of many MLM products make a true transfer sale impossible. People do indeed need shampoo. But how many people are willing to trade their usual $5 brand for a new shampoo that costs five times as much? Len noticed immediately that Longevity's products had prices similar to those you would find in a retail store, making them perfect transfer products. And there were so many of them—52 products in all!

"I immediately got on the phone with the other guys," says Len, "and told them, 'You've really got to see this one.'"

The School of Hard Knocks

Jim and Adi Song had started off years before with a company called American 3D, selling 3-D (three-dimensional) cameras through network marketing. After three years in business, they had achieved annual sales of $63 million. Unfortunately, the 3-D photo technology required a unique development process, which limited the Songs to just a few chemical suppliers. When one of their key suppliers started shipping inferior developing solutions, the quality of the photos plummeted instantly, sending the distributors into an angry uproar.

American 3D subsequently won a multimillion-dollar lawsuit against the supplier (now being appealed), but the victory came too late. The Songs had lost their distributors and their momentum in the marketplace. They had, however, come out of the ordeal with one hard lesson: *never stake your company on a single product.*

The Songs reorganized their company. But this time they planned to hit the market on a wide front. They put together a team of top authorities in health and nutrition to design a complete line of high-quality nutritional, skin care, weight management, and beauty products.

Infrastructure

When the Songs relaunched their company as Longevity Network, Ltd. in April 1994, the company had one other key advantage over most of its MLM rivals. It had the entire infrastructure of American 3D still in place, including 40 computer workstations, sufficient phone lines and equipment to handle $100 million a year in orders, in-house graphic arts and design departments, office space, and a massive warehouse.

This meant that no matter how fast Longevity grew, it would never experience the sort of growing pains that afflicted the FreeStylers' first company. With tens of thousands of dollars less overhead per month than most MLM companies, Longevity was well-insulated against the top two killers of network marketing startups—undercapitalization and inadequate infrastructure to handle rapid growth. The FreeStylers had found a new home.

A Mysterious Phone Call

One brisk November day, after several months in the business, Len Clements received a mysterious phone call from Jim Song. Jim was holding a meeting with a core group of five leaders at company headquarters in Henderson, Nevada. The subject of the meeting was so confidential that none of the participants would even be told what it was about until they got off the plane in Henderson. As you can imagine, it was a long plane ride for Len, filled with fear and foreboding. But, when he arrived, Len was relieved and delighted to discover that the purpose of the meeting was to straighten out one of the company's most nagging problems—its compensation plan.

A Perception Problem

Over the last several months, while the FreeStylers had been recruiting for Longevity, their results had been good but not spectacular. Among the chief obstacles, they felt, was a serious perception problem. Although Longevity employed a very fair compensation plan, many prospects with experience in network marketing *perceived* it to be a difficult plan, for various technical reasons.

The FreeStylers were not alone in that perception. Two and a half months earlier, Jim and Adi Song had conducted a brainstorming meeting in Los Angeles, during which they had milked Longevity's 55 top leaders for advice and input. They had received an almost unanimous message from the field that the comp plan needed revising. Now they were going ahead and implementing the distributors' wishes.

Resistance

"Tell us what you like and what you don't like about the plan," the Songs urged the core group at the meeting. "What do you want us to change? What would you like us to keep?"

During the meeting, Jim and Adi Song put a white board at the head of the room and drew two columns on it. As they discussed each type of compensation plan in turn, they would list the pros and cons in the two columns.

"When we got to binary plans," says Len, "there was a great deal of apprehension. The general consensus seemed to be, 'Let's not even talk about binaries. This isn't an option.'"

In other companies, with less mature management, such resistance might have aroused hostility and rancor—especially since it turned out that Jim Song was personally enamored of the binary plan. But Jim took a more constructive approach. He challenged the naysayers to make a list of all the things they didn't like about binary plans.

"It took us about an hour and a half to make that list," says Len.

"Okay," said Jim, when they had finished. "Now go nuts. Design what you would consider your dream binary plan. Don't worry about the payout or the company's share or anything else. Do whatever you have to do to make every one of your objections go away."

The Binary Craze

In a binary plan, each distributor has two people on his first level, and beneath those two people are two separate legs—a "left" leg and a "right" leg. At the end of each week, the computer tabulates how much volume has occurred in each leg and pays a commission based on the total volume in the "weak" leg—the leg with less sales volume.

From the time they were introduced in 1989, binaries quickly developed into a craze. Their allure lies in the fact that in a binary plan, you get paid on the total volume of the leg rather than just a few levels of it. This is a welcome contrast to other plans that place severe limits on the number of people in your "pay range." If you're in a seven-level "unilevel" plan (a popular configuration for MLM comp plans), for example, and you recruit a heavy hitter onto your eighth level, then that heavy hitter falls below your pay range, so no matter how huge an organization he builds, you make no money from it. In a binary plan, you can place that heavy hitter on your 20th level or your 100th and still make your percentage from his sales volume.

The Catch

Unfortunately, Len contends, much of the attraction of binaries is based on a slew of misperceptions. Like any other plan, binaries can be easy or hard to work, depending on the individual plan. But many companies have imposed heavy *breakage* on their binary plans, making it difficult for the average distributor to earn significant money from them.

"There's a perception out there," says Len, "that stairstep breakaways are tough and binaries are easy. But, in fact, most of the binaries I've seen have far more breakage than the average stairstep breakaway. They're just better at hiding it."

"Runaway Legs"

Most of the breakage in binary plans occurs in so-called "runaway legs." This happens when one leg of your organization dramatically outperforms the other leg. In an extreme case, you might end up with one leg doing, say, $50,000 per week and another doing zero. Because binary plans pay only on the "weak" leg, you will get zero commission. And no matter how hard you try to catch up to your strong leg by focusing your recruiting efforts on your weak leg, you'll probably never succeed. The strong leg will always stay ahead, because it has more manpower to work with. That's why it's called a runaway leg.

Incremental Payouts

Another source of breakage in binaries, according to Len, is the practice of "incremental payouts." Instead of paying a straight percentage of total sales volume, they pay on set increments of sales volume. Let's say your plan pays a

20 percent commission. If your sales volume for the week is $1,900, you would expect to make $380.

But, in most binaries, you won't. That's because $1,900 falls *between* the two set increments of $1,000 and $2,000. The company rounds off your volume to the lowest of the two increments—in this case, $1,000—and pays you 20 percent of that: $200 instead of the $380 you expected. Theoretically, the remaining $900 gets "carried over" into next week's paycheck, but, in practice, there's always a certain amount of money that remains hovering in limbo, "carried over" from week to week but somehow never managing to find its way from the company's bank account into yours.

Plug up the Breakage

The list goes on. In the end, the brainstorming group managed to identify myriad ways that binary plans impose breakage. When they finally sat down to compose their "dream" binary plan, they systematically plugged up each of these cash leaks.

They dispensed with the runaway leg problem by instituting a "matching bonus" that allowed people to get paid on their strong leg as well as their weak one. They abolished incremental payouts in favor of a flat percentage of all volume in the weak leg. In the end, each and every one of the various forms of binary breakage was "plugged up." To Len's amazement, Jim and Adi Song were not only delighted with the plan, but added a few flourishes of their own and decided to use it for Longevity Network.

Counterrevolution

Albert Einstein warned that "Great spirits always encounter violent opposition from mediocre minds."

The dream team at Longevity Network proved no exception to this rule. The plan they had drawn up was not only revolutionary—it was downright dangerous to many companies, whose binary plans continued to impose heavy breakage. These companies had long justified their plans to their distributors by arguing that without so much breakage, the company would hemorrhage cash and go out of business.

Now, all of a sudden, here was a company claiming that its binary plan paid up to twice the commissions as the others. Nasty rumors began circulating—some of them, Len suspects, spread by competing binary companies—that Longevity was about to go bankrupt because its plan was unworkable. You simply couldn't pay out so much money on a binary plan and stay in business, the rumormongers insisted.

Mass Defections

The rumors did their work. For three months, the top leaders in competing binary companies stayed where they were, keeping a hopeful—but suspicious—watch over Longevity Network. Nevertheless, they couldn't afford to wait long. In the hotly competitive arena of binary companies, these leaders knew they would have trouble keeping their downlines loyal if a rival binary offered a better deal.

"After three months, they saw that we were still in business," says Len. "We were still coming out with more product and we were still paying checks on time or even early. As soon as they realized the new plan wasn't bankrupting the company, the binary people started moving over en masse. We had leaders with downlines of 4,000 to 13,000 people suddenly moving over to Longevity from other binary companies."

The Innovation Curve

During the seven months prior to changing its comp plan, Longevity Network's downline grew at a good but undistinguished rate of five percent per month. But after changing to the "dream" binary plan in November 1995, its monthly growth rate skyrocketed to 50 percent. By January, the FreeStyles Group's organization doubled in size.

In the long-run, Longevity's comp-plan advantage is likely to be temporary. Even Len admits that some competing binary companies are rushing to imitate many of the most attractive features of Longevity's plan. If the history of the industry provides any indication, the analysis of binaries in this chapter may well be obsolete within a few months or a couple of years.

"Comp plans have always evolved by leapfrogging each other," says Len.

Nevertheless, as long as Jim and Adi Song keep an open door and an open ear to innovators like the FreeStyles Group, it seems likely they will stay solidly on the crest of the Wave-Three Revolution for many years to come.

LEADER BREEDERS

Unfortunately, not every company recognizes the value of forward-looking leaders like Kate Gill-Grossi and Len Clements. Some network marketing CEOs, locked in the habits and rituals of Wave-Two thinking, will even tend to look upon such innovators as pests and nuisances. But for those select few who aren't afraid to upset the corporate applecart, the talents and vision of today's Wave-Three leaders offer a cornucopia of untapped opportunity.

Indeed, enlightened companies go to great lengths to set themselves up as *leader breeders*—environments that attract and nurture innovative leaders and provide long-term incentives to keep them loyal. By employing such a strategy, a company called Rexall Showcase not only saved itself from disaster but seized a commanding position on the frontline of 21st-century network marketing.

A Modern-Day Daniel Boone

Todd Smith was a restless soul. He was to entrepreneur-
ship in the 1990s what Daniel Boone was to the old Kentucky frontier. Legend has it that Daniel Boone would
pack up and move further west every time the neighbors
got so close he could see the smoke from their chimneys.
Similarly, Todd Smith would think nothing of abandoning
the most successful business if he sensed that the cutting
edge of profit and innovation had moved elsewhere.

Six months out of high school, Todd started a silk-
screening business that in four years achieved a sales volume of a million dollars a year. But when he saw he could
make higher margins in residential real estate, the 22-
year-old entrepreneur abandoned silk-screening without
a second thought. Four and a half years later, Todd had
sold 430 homes for over $46 million and become one of the
top producing real estate agents in the country, making
over $400,000 a year.

More Leverage

In 1990, the Wave-Three Revolution was just beginning
to pick up steam. It was in that year that Todd, like millions of others around the country, first heard the words
network marketing. The concept captivated him instantly.
Todd saw that no other business offered so much leverage
for the same time and effort expended. Once more, Todd
pulled up stakes and headed for the frontier. He joined a
fast-growing skin care company that seemed to offer
plenty of room for growth.

A Sales Superstar

Todd thrived in his new company. During his first presentation, he had 38 people in the room and sponsored nine

of them. Four months later, he was packing 400 people at a time into his weekly business briefings and pulling over $30,000 per month in commissions.

"I built an organization in 16 months that spanned the country and had more than 10,000 distributors," says Todd.

The Cutting Edge

But, in a short time, Todd began to glimpse the proverbial smoke from his neighbor's chimney. In many respects, his company was on the cutting edge of the Wave-Three Revolution. Todd had the highest respect for the professionalism of the company's owners and top managers and for their commitment to producing a quality product. But he realized that in one crucial area the company had fallen behind the innovation curve—the breakneck race among Wave-Three companies to provide ever-more-innovative ways of making the business easier for the average distributor to work.

Its compensation plan reeked of Wave-Two thinking.

The plan was tough. Real tough. Just to earn the right to pull a modest 14 percent commission, a distributor had to maintain up to $3,000 in monthly sales volume for five straight months. After attaining the coveted "executive" status, then, you could easily lose it and have to start all over again simply because you failed to maintain your $3,000 volume for two months.

What's Good for Your Downline Is Good for You

For high-powered entrepreneurs like Todd, the plan offered lucrative payouts on the back end. But, for the average person, Todd realized its conditions were overly harsh.

"The average person in this country is barely willing to work this week to get paid next Friday," says Todd. "I found that most people in my downline were simply not willing to wait six months to get paid. In network marketing, you have to choose a plan that works not only for you but also for the average person in your downline."

During the Wave-Two era, high qualifications and stiff penalties for nonperformance were the norm. But, as 1991 dawned on the MLM industry, a new mood was in the air. More and more companies were experimenting with plans that paid off for the part-timer as well as for the heavy hitter. Todd sensed the opening of a new frontier. Slinging his proverbial musket and powder horn over his shoulder, Todd set off across the Kentucky hills in search of greener pastures and wider elbow room.

A Distribution Visionary

Paradoxically, Todd Smith was destined to find his new frontier in a company that was more than 90 years old. Rexall drugstores had been a fixture on American main streets since 1903. But, after falling on hard times in the mid-80s, the venerable brand name went on the selling block. In 1985, it was purchased by an entrepreneur named Carl DeSantis.

Carl shared a lot of qualities with Todd Smith. Like Todd, he was a pioneer. From his modest salary as a drugstore manager and a $6,000 second mortgage on his house, Carl had started a mail-order vitamin company out of his bedroom, bringing in women from his local Catholic church to take calls and pack orders for minimum wage. Carl was a visionary. He realized, before most other business leaders, that efficient distribution was the next frontier.

An Unexpected Success

"People told me it was the wrong time to get into the vitamin business," says Carl, "but I saw that the competition didn't ship in a timely fashion, they ran out of stock, and their prices were too high. I knew I could do better."

From its modest beginnings, Sundown Vitamins, Inc. grew to a $13 million company in seven years. By 1985— nine years after starting his business—Carl DeSantis was wealthy enough to acquire the famous Rexall brand name in a multimillion-dollar deal.

An Experiment

"Rexall was a powerful name," says Carl. "To millions of people, it conveyed trust, good health, and wellness."

Carl decided to leverage that trust into a bold experiment in distribution. Carl knew that ad copy on a package could never explain the complex biochemical benefits of many of the health, nutrition, and weight-loss products he planned to bring out under the Rexall brand name. To tell his story, he needed far more than the five seconds or less most customers take to make a buying decision in a store.

"You can't tell a story from a store shelf," says Carl. But MLM distributors could do it face to face with their customers. For years, Carl had watched the success of network marketing companies such as Amway and Herbalife. Although Carl was well aware of the sleazy image MLM had acquired during the Wave-One and Wave-Two eras, he felt that Rexall's reassuring aura would generate sufficient goodwill in the marketplace to enable Carl to launch a new kind of network marketing company based on professionalism and high ethics. In 1990, Carl made his move, creating a new MLM subsidiary called Rexall Showcase.

Wave-Two Management

But Carl DeSantis's bold new experiment was not destined for a rose-strewn path. From opening day, things went rapidly from bad to worse. His inexperience in network marketing forced Carl to rely on outside help. He went through two presidents in one year, both successful MLM distributors who had never held a corporate job. Under their loose, Wave-Two management, many distributors ran rampant, frontloading new recruits and making unauthorized medical claims for products.

"At first, we were attracting the sort of people who were not interested in building for the long term," says Damon DeSantis, Carl's son, who is now president of Rexall Showcase. "We had some good ones, but a lot of them were the sort who just wanted to make a quick hit."

Bleeding Cash

Meanwhile, expenses mounted perilously. As the company poured millions into sales tools and computer systems, the Rexall Showcase division quickly became a financial albatross.

For the first few months of 1991, the division did only $40,000 per month in sales, while bleeding up to ten times that amount every month. It wasn't long before Carl woke up one day to realize he had invested $5 million in Rexall Showcase without seeing a penny in profit.

A Wave-Three Comp Plan

Despite these setbacks, Rexall Showcase possessed one crucial advantage that, in the end, would outweigh every problem: It had a Wave-Three compensation plan.

Even as it rolled and churned through the turbulent waters of its first year, Rexall had already attracted the attention of a group of forward-looking leaders in Todd Smith's company, among them Steve Campbell, Randy Schroeder, and Stewart Hughes. Like Todd, these men were looking for a company with a cutting-edge comp plan, one that would make it easy for part-timers and average people to build a business.

The three of them met with Carl DeSantis at Rexall Sundown headquarters in Boca Raton, Florida, and they liked what they heard. On the flight back home, the team asked themselves, "If there were any one person we could bring with us to Rexall from our company, who would it be?"

"Todd Smith" was the name that sprang immediately to every pair of lips. Before the plane even landed, Todd got a phone call. He had been drafted.

A Solemn Promise

The picture could not have been grimmer than it was when Todd and the other leaders came onboard in September 1991. There were very few products available. After a year in business, Rexall Showcase was still hemorrhaging twice as much cash as it made every month. Each time the executive committee for the parent company met to discuss their fledgling MLM subsidiary, they spoke darkly of "throwing good money after bad" and "cutting our losses."

Todd knew he was taking an incredible risk by walking away from a five-figure monthly income at his old company. But Carl DeSantis took him aside and made him a solemn promise.

"I know you're making a big commitment to come here," said Carl. "I know you'll be leaving a lot of money behind. But you've got my word that I will not let you down."

A Winning Team

Carl DeSantis proved as good as his word. He let the executive committee know that "cutting our losses" was not an option and that the new group of leaders would be given a chance to prove themselves. He also appointed his son, Damon, as the new president for Rexall Showcase. Damon had been the most vocal supporter of the network marketing program from the beginning. He had researched the industry and had helped persuade the executive committee that an MLM subsidiary was viable. Since the beginning, Damon had served as the corporate liaison between Rexall Showcase and the parent company.

"I had been watching over this division from the beginning, through two different presidents," says Damon, "and I had learned a great deal about what to do and what not to do."

Division of Labor

One of the chief lessons Damon had learned was to enforce a strict division of labor. The parent company would stick to what it did best—developing and producing a line of high-quality health and nutrition products. The leaders would be given a free hand to do what they were good at—recruiting and training a top distributor force.

The new leaders proved worthy of Damon's trust. Discipline and professionalism were the new watchwords for the Rexall field force. The frontloading and unauthorized product claims that had plagued the field force in its early days never returned. On his end, Damon focused on churning out quality products, such as a new line of homeopathic remedies, an energizing tonic called Invigorol, and a toothpaste called Orarex that fights gum disease. For the first time since Rexall Showcase began, it had a winning team in place. The results followed soon after.

A Dramatic Turnaround

Things turned around rapidly. In his third month, Todd Smith alone generated over $300,000 in sales volume—

one-fifth of the entire company's volume in its first year. By the first quarter of 1993, Rexall Showcase was running in the black, and, four years after its founding, it was growing twice as fast as Carl DeSantis's mail-order and retail divisions. Sales for Rexall Showcase exceeded $75 million in the 1995–96 fiscal year.

A Unique Incentive Plan

Today, Rexall appears to have entered a growth cycle that will last for many years. Nevertheless, the DeSantises understand that the long-term loyalty of their top distributors is contingent upon their ability as a company to keep moving briskly along the innovation curve. With that goal in mind, the DeSantises recently announced a unique incentive plan. In February 1996, Rexall became the first network marketing company ever to offer a stock purchase and stock option plan to qualified distributors.

Taking a Page from the Fortune 500

Fortune 500 corporations have long used stock options to motivate executives. The potential cash value of such perks is considerable. If, for example, your company issues you an option to purchase 2,000 shares of stock at the current market price of, say, $27 per share, by the time you choose to exercise your option, the stock may have doubled or even tripled in price. You can then buy 2,000 shares at the original price of $27 for a profit of well over $100,000. And you don't have to risk a penny out of your pocket while you're waiting for the stock to rise.

In corporate America, such offers are used not only to give executives an owner's perspective on the company's operations but also to keep them from jumping ship. The longer they stay around, the more money their option is worth. Many companies enhance this effect by doling out their stock options bit by bit through a "vesting" schedule that may span five years or more—a stratagem that Rexall has shrewdly adopted in its program.

Building Wealth

"Now our top distributors are not only working for that monthly check," says Damon, "but they're also participating in a wealth-building plan over and above the marketing plan."

Those Rexall distributors who qualify (you must have at least four active legs in your organization) can now gain equity not only in the MLM division but in the entire corporate entity of Rexall Sundown, including its mail-order, wholesale, and international divisions. Damon believes this will offer a much-needed supplement to the retirement plans of MLM leaders.

Every heavy hitter dreams of retiring after ten years or so with a hefty residual income. But, all too often, these early retirees find that their sales volume slacks off the moment they take their hand from the tiller. Their downlines may keep producing for many years, but usually not at the same level they produced under the retiree's direct leadership. Damon suggests that the equity Rexall distributors earn will help make up for that anticipated fall in income.

"This is a calling card to the new breed of professionals who are looking at network marketing today," says Damon. "People from corporate America understand options. They understand stock. They understand equity. Now, when you go to recruit somebody who is used to being a corporate vice president, you have a story to tell that really catches their ear."

The Next Frontier

As for Todd Smith, he appreciates the extra motivation the stock option plan provides. Since starting with Rexall, Todd has personally earned over $4 million. It would be easy for him to become complacent. But the new program gives Todd a reason to keep pushing.

"I've already tapped out the comp plan," he says. "I'm making the highest commissions now that our plan will pay out. But now they're giving me an incentive to go out and work harder so I can qualify for bigger stock options. It gives people like me a new level to strive for."

THE FREE MARKET

As leaders leap from one company to another—bringing their reputations, their influence, and often their downlines with them—MLM companies are under constant pressure to become leader breeders. Far more than the sporadic and often wrongheaded intervention of government regulators, this competitive pressure keeps the industry in a state of creative flux, in which companies strive every day to remake themselves to become more profitable, more fair, more honest, and more enticing to heavy hitters and rank-and-file distributors alike. That's the free-market way of "regulating" the industry. It also happens to be the Wave Three Way.

Chapter 11

FIND YOUR DREAM SPONSOR

A ll you need to get started in this program is $300,"
the man explained. "That's not a problem, is it?"
Freddie Rick sighed. It was a problem, but
Freddie didn't know quite how to admit that to his friend.
In fact, Freddie had only $1 in his pocket, the whole of his
worldly wealth. The only reason Freddie had even agreed
to come to this meeting at all was that his friend had
promised to buy him lunch afterward. And Freddie was in
no position to turn down a free lunch.

With an ironic smile, Freddie replied, "I guess $300
won't be a problem. At the moment, though, I'm about
$299 short."

Freddie's friend gave him a long, hard look. When he
finally spoke, he said something that Freddie did not expect but that he would remember for the rest of his life.

"I don't want you to take this the wrong way," said his
friend, "but, buddy, if you don't even have $300, then
something you're doing just isn't working."

A Flawed Strategy

Freddie left in a huff and spent the next two days sulking.
But beneath his anger, Freddie knew in his heart that
his friend was right. Something was wrong with his life

strategy. Terribly wrong. In his high school yearbook, right beneath his senior picture, Freddie had announced his intention to become a millionaire by the year 1999. With only nine years left before his deadline, Freddie couldn't possibly be farther from his goal.

Take One Step

Yet, even as he sulked over his friend's criticism, Freddie experienced an insight that was destined to change his life. Freddie realized that if he wanted to make a million in nine years, he would have to start *right now*. That didn't mean he had to hit on a million-dollar idea or launch a million-dollar business on the spot. But it did mean he had to get started by taking at least *one small step* in the right direction.

Even if he took only very tiny steps, Freddie reasoned, their effect would build up over time. The reverse was also true. Freddie feared that, if he kept on going in the same rut, the years would pass before he knew it, and 1999 would find him just as broke, just as desperate, and ten times as bitter as he was today.

A Gnawing Hunger

All his life, Freddie Rick had hungered for greatness.

"I knew I was put here to be somebody, to achieve something," he says. "I just didn't know how or what."

In the Marine Corps, Freddie was a sniper, highly trained in the arts of concealment, stealth, and marksmanship. But, after his discharge, Freddie found few jobs available for someone with his unique qualifications—few jobs that were legal, anyway.

At first, Freddie worked in a Burger King. But he always kept a watchful eye out for opportunities. At one point, he invented a device called the Chip Stick that peeled potatoes. He even lined up a distributor who agreed to advance him money. But the deal fell through when Freddie found that a competing inventor had already gotten the patent.

Next, he started a carpet cleaning business. Freddie placed the hopeful sign "Millionaire in Training" on the license plate holder of his truck. But the business soon went broke, and Freddie with it.

Course Correction

Like a ship that has wandered off course, Freddie sensed that he was drifting into strange and hostile waters. His intentions were good, but his methods were obviously ineffective. Freddie was badly in need of a midcourse correction.

It was just then that Freddie allowed his friend to drag him to an opportunity meeting for an MLM company. Although he had only come along for the free lunch, Freddie's ears pricked up when the speaker started talking about geometric growth and residual income. It made sense to him. Freddie suspected he could do well at this business. But, without $300 to get started, Freddie knew it was only a pipe dream.

After sulking for two days, Freddie took action. He went down to a pawn shop near his apartment in San Diego and pawned every item of value that he owned. It didn't amount to much. Freddie pawned his 9-millimeter pistol ("Every good sniper's got one of those," he says), some carpet cleaning equipment, and a 14-carat gold ring that his father had given him years ago. For the lot, Freddie got only $325. But that was enough to get him started in his first network marketing business.

In Search of a Mentor

In his new company, Freddie searched hard for a mentor—an older and wiser head who could keep him on course and warn him when he went adrift. But Freddie searched in vain. Those who had time for him gave him poor advice. And those whose advice he respected wouldn't give him time.

On one occasion, Freddie boldly approached one of the company's top distributors at a convention. He asked the man very humbly if he would do a three-way call with him so Freddie could learn his prospecting techniques. The man fixed Freddie with a cold eye.

"Son, you're not even in my downline," he said at last. "I have no monetary interest in you whatsoever. You need to find somebody who does."

Freddie felt as if he had swallowed a ball of ice. As he slunk away into the crowd, his face burned with embarrassment.

"If I ever make it and become successful in this business," Freddie vowed to himself, "I will never be like that man."

Bad Advice

So Freddie kept drifting farther and farther off course. The only people who would talk to him were those with a "monetary interest" in him. And their monetary interest invariably lay in pressuring Freddie to buy more and more inventory every month.

Like all too many MLM firms during the Wave-Two era, the company Freddie had joined tended to reward distributors for buying huge quantities of product each month—on company credit, if they wished. The higher your monthly purchases, the larger commission you were awarded. After a year and a half, Freddie was earning the highest possible commissions in the company. Unfortunately, his "success" did not put money in his pocket. Freddie soon found himself with a highfalutin title, $150,000 in debt, and little or no income. His foray into network marketing had been a disaster.

Steady As She Goes

At the age of 24, Freddie was deep in debt and farther than ever from his goal. Unable to afford a real apartment, he stayed with an artist friend who had set up a live-in studio in a warehouse. There, Freddie eked out a tenuous living as a nightclub bouncer.

For all appearances, Freddie was at his lowest ebb, scrounging on the very fringes of society. Yet, he was more hopeful now than ever. In leaving that company behind, Freddie had taken an important step in getting himself back on course. He'd taken some lumps, but he had learned some valuable lessons too. No matter how the storms blew or the waves drove, Freddie knew that as long as he stayed on course, he would one day sail proudly into port.

A Lingering Taste

Most people in Freddie's position would have rejected network marketing entirely. But one of the lessons Freddie had learned is that MLM works, if you do it right. Some months at the company, Freddie had received checks for $20,000 or more. Other months, he'd gotten nothing. But the taste of those big checks lingered long in his mouth, and Freddie was determined to get them back. Night after night, Freddie lay on his mattress in his friend's warehouse studio, playing and replaying his favorite training tapes from the company he'd left, and dreaming of his next MLM opportunity.

The Secret

Freddie's favorite training tapes were those by Jeff Olson, one of the leading distributors at his old company. Many times, Freddie had tried to work up the nerve to approach Jeff and seek his help. But it never seemed quite the right time.

Unlike Freddie, Jeff hadn't gone into debt. He'd worked the same opportunity and made good money at it. Jeff knew The Secret. When Freddie listened to his tapes, he felt an invisible bond that was hard to explain.

"He wasn't fake," says Freddie. "I could tell that from his tapes and trainings. Whether you liked it or not, you always knew where he stood. A lot of people, when they get money, they forget how to relate to the little guy. But Jeff never forgot where he came from. He always had a way of reaching out to the average person without talking down."

The more he listened to Jeff Olson's tapes, the more clearly a plan formed in Freddie's mind. One way or another, Freddie thought, he would find an opportunity to apprentice himself to this man. Jeff Olson would be his mentor. Jeff Olson would teach him The Secret.

HUMBLE BEGINNINGS

When Freddie first saw him speak, Jeff Olson exuded the polish and poise of a Fortune 100 executive. He talked business and finance like a Harvard professor. He had money, style, and brains. But Jeff had not started out that way.

As a boy, Jeff Olson seemed headed for failure. His father died when Jeff was only 10, leaving him moody and rebellious. He subsequently never got above a C average in school. His third-grade teacher told him he had a low IQ. "The only thing I was good at," says Jeff, "was getting in trouble."

By the time Jeff finished high school, practically the only person who still believed in him was his mother—and Jeff gave her very little reason to keep believing. After managing to get into college by the skin of his teeth, Jeff made a consistent D average through his entire first year. He thereupon left school and made his way to Daytona Beach, Florida, where Jeff became, in his own words, "a professional beach bum."

A Single Daily Discipline

Growing his hair long and curly, Jeff soon acquired the nickname of "Gorgeous George"—a professional wrestler known for his golden locks and comely mien. Jeff augmented his macho image with a rigorous program of weight lifting. Pumping iron every day, Jeff built himself up to 230 pounds of solid beef, with arms like pile drivers. The girls loved it. But Jeff's daily workouts produced another effect, which Jeff had never anticipated.

In a life appallingly devoid of discipline, Jeff's vanity had lured him, quite by accident, into a baptism of rigor and toil. Each time he sat down at the Nautilus machine, Jeff's muscles cried out for rest but received only punishment. With each heave of the weights, his willpower hardened like stone. Each morning, when Jeff looked in the mirror to shave, his eyes gleamed back with just a little more steel than the day before.

The Change

The change had been building in Jeff for weeks. When it finally came, it struck like a sledgehammer. It happened one day at work, while Jeff was mowing the greens at the local country club. He paused for a moment, gazing off at the club patrons far across the greens, leaning against their golf carts and swinging their clubs with long, lazy strokes. Then it hit him like a tidal wave, a flood of nauseous emotion, like bile burning its way up his gullet.

How come I'm over here sweating in cutoffs, asked a molten voice from deep inside, *and they're over there wearing nice clothes and having a great time? Why do they have it a hundred times better than me? Do they work a hundred times harder? Are they a hundred times smarter?*

"No," came the answer. "I'm just as good as those guys. In fact, I'm better. I don't have to be a bum. I can get out of this."

For the first time since his father died, Jeff had seen himself with crystal clarity. What he saw disgusted him. Shortly thereafter, he loaded up his 1964 Dodge Dart and took off for home.

Whiz Kid

"I begged my way back into college," says Jeff.

Now that Jeff had changed his attitude, the "low IQ" of which his third-grade teacher had accused him mysteriously ceased to be an obstacle. Indeed, Jeff went on to become something of a whiz kid, getting straight A's his very first semester. With a challenging load of marketing and economics courses, Jeff graduated near the top of his class at the University of New Mexico and was hired straight out of school by Texas Instruments.

The Next Step

By the time Jeff Olson joined his first network marketing company, he had tasted a broader spectrum of success—and failure—than most people can imagine in a lifetime. By age 28, Jeff had ridden the corporate fast track as far as it would go and had left to start his own business. By age 33 he had made and lost his first million, having built the fifth largest solar energy company in the country, only to have his legs cut out from under him when the government slashed Jeff's tax credits. It forced him to shut down his business.

Jeff was already on the rebound, building a group of advertising and direct marketing companies, when an old friend of his wife's handed him an audiotape about a new MLM opportunity. At first, Jeff was apathetic. It was three months (and about 40 phone calls from his wife's friend) before Jeff finally listened to the tape. But when he did, Jeff was stunned by what he learned. The company was grossing over $300 million in annual sales through word-of-mouth marketing alone.

In a flash, Jeff saw the future. Certain that he had discovered the next phase of his business evolution, Jeff joined the new company. Only a few months later, his downline had grown so dramatically that Jeff dissolved his other companies and went full-time into network marketing.

The New Breed

Back in the Wave-Two era, Jeff Olson's corporate and marketing background made him an oddity in the MLM world. Industry old-timers lured recruits by showing off paychecks and boasting about their flashy new cars. Jeff, on the other hand, pulled out pie charts and bell curves to buttress his prospecting talks. Within a few years, Jeff's sophisticated style would become the industry norm. But back in 1990, Jeff was among the very first of the New Breed.

"My business background enabled me to present the opportunity in terms that were familiar and plausible to the average businessperson," says Jeff. "I was able to attract people that other network marketers could never attract, by convincing them that this was a viable form of distribution."

Within the first year and a half, Jeff rose to the top one-tenth of one percent of the company in terms of sales volume. Tens of thousands strong, his downline was built not from the usual grab bag of MLM junkies but from business leaders and white-collar professionals.

A Bad Conscience

Jeff leveraged his business background to the hilt. But there was another side of Jeff that also cried out to be heard. It was a part that Jeff had tried very hard to forget, a part that he thought was safely tucked away in the past. But now, at the peak of Jeff's success, his hidden side that still remembered poverty, desperation, and failure began to make itself heard. It tugged at his conscience every day and gave him no rest.

As a network marketer, Jeff saw a lot of pain in his work. Although he hadn't yet met Freddie Rick, Jeff had seen a thousand people just like him. Day after day, he saw them lining up like ducks in a shooting gallery, their eyes brimming with hope and their heads filled with perky slogans by self-help gurus such as Napoleon Hill. He saw them pour their lives, their money, and their dreams into MLM opportunities, only to creep away a few months later with their heads hung low and their pockets turned inside out.

Jeff knew that network marketing worked. He knew that the theory was sound. But in practice it continued to fail too many people. Jeff began to ponder what it would really take to transform MLM so that it might work for the Freddie Ricks as well as it already had for the Jeff Olsons. Night after night, as he lay in the dark, Jeff worried and chewed at this question like a bull terrier. When the answer finally came to him, it would transform not only Jeff's life, but the lives of tens of thousands across America.

What If?

One morning, as Jeff Olson was waiting to catch an early plane at the Phoenix airport, he stopped to get his shoes shined. A friendly woman in her mid-40s ran the shoe shine stand. As she buffed Jeff's shoes, she chatted brightly, turning now and then to exchange jokes and pleasantries with the janitors and maintenance men passing by. As Jeff watched her, a strange thought entered his head.

What would this woman's life be like today if she had taken a different path five years ago? he wondered.

The woman seemed bright and well-spoken. She carried herself well. With some sharp clothes and a stylish hairdo, Jeff could easily have imagined her as a successful businesswoman. Then Jeff noticed the book she'd been reading.

"It was some trashy novel," he recalls. "There was a small pile of them sitting next to the chair."

Suppose this woman had spent the last five years reading books like Napoleon Hill's *Think and Grow Rich* and Stephen Covey's *Seven Habits of Highly Effective People,* thought Jeff. Suppose she had spent those years making friends with people who were going places in life, instead of hobnobbing with janitors. Where would she be now?

Slaves and Drudges

Long after he left the shoe shine stand, these questions rolled over and over in Jeff's mind. They haunted him as he studied the faces thronging the terminal—faces clouded with worry and boredom, faces bowed with exhaustion, faces red with anger and pain. These were not the faces of free men and women, Jeff realized, but of slaves, drudges, and automatons. In that moment, a sadness pierced Jeff's heart so suddenly and deeply that he nearly gasped from the force of it.

"I felt for a moment as if I were going to cry," says Jeff.

A Support Structure

What struck Jeff in that instant was the needlessness of so much human suffering. Here, in the richest country in the world—where every bookstore brimmed with motivational tomes by the finest coaches from Dale Carnegie to Earl Nightingale—only the tiniest sliver of humanity ever seemed to learn how it felt to achieve their dreams. The rest slogged through life like serfs beneath the lash, their eyes burning with envy and fear.

What they lacked, Jeff realized, was a support system. Neither their jobs, schools, families, nor TV sets were telling them how to break out of the rut. Like ships cast adrift in the sea, they wandered off course with no pilot to guide them. But what if that guidance could be provided? What if it became possible to create an infrastructure, a support system, whereby people could gain access to that life-giving information now languishing unread on bookstore shelves?

"I envisioned something almost like a church," says Jeff, "an environment and a community that was conducive to change, that would bring self-help information right into people's homes, where people would constantly be spurred to improve how they thought, what they read, with whom they associated."

A Kindred Spirit

Very early in his MLM career, Jeff had befriended a fellow distributor named Eric Worre, who seemed to share his concerns about "the little guy." Through many long, rambling conversations, Jeff and Eric explored the secrets of success and pondered the causes of failure.

At one point, they spent four days holed up in a resort in Scottsdale, Arizona, brainstorming and taking notes, while a tape recorder ran in the background. During that single long weekend, they drew up a business plan for a truly revolutionary company—a network marketing firm that sold not the usual "lotions and potions," but self-help teachings in the form of books, tapes, and videos from the leading personal development gurus of the day.

The Slight Edge

The guiding philosophy of this company, Jeff and Eric decided, would be something they called the Slight Edge. Winners clearly had an "edge" over losers. But it was only a *slight* edge. Indeed, it was just as easy to succeed in life as it was to fail. Maybe easier.

"It only takes five years to turn your life completely around," says Jeff. "But it will take you the rest of your life to fail."

According to Jeff and Eric, success comes not through great feats of exertion but through a hundred insignificant decisions we make every day. These decisions are easy to make. They are also easy *not* to make. It's easy to order a health salad. But it's also easy to order junk food. The junk food may ultimately kill you. But the salads will leave you sleek, svelte, and glowing with health. Either way, the Slight Edge is always at work, either for you or against you.

Insignificant Choices

The reason so many people choose failure, Jeff and Eric concluded, is that the hundreds of insignificant choices we make everyday don't affect us *immediately*. We don't get a heart attack the moment we swallow our French fries. Nor do we shed 30 pounds the instant we down a niçoise salad. In the short term, the effects are invisible and therefore easy to ignore.

But in the self-help community Jeff and Eric envisioned, people would receive daily reminders of their long-term goals from friends, family, colleagues, and media. They would never be able to forget the far-reaching effects of their daily, "insignificant" actions. The Slight Edge would work for them rather than against them. And they would succeed at a rate unheard of in ordinary society.

The Hand of Fate

At that point, Jeff Olson still did not know that Freddie Rick existed. But he would find out soon enough. Fate had woven their lives together in a fabric of exceeding richness and strangeness. The loom on which it accomplished this work turned out to be a new MLM company called Quorum.

Quorum sold electronic security systems for cars and homes. To Jeff, it seemed a perfect product. It had always bothered Jeff that his present company seemed more effective at loading distributors down with inventory than it did at selling products to end users. At times, Jeff felt its core business amounted to little more than shifting inventory from a big warehouse to a lot of little warehouses—the garages of hapless distributors like Freddie Rick. Jeff thought that Quorum had a better plan for moving product at retail. He thought the little guy would stand a better chance in such a company. And so, in September 1992, Jeff ended his relationship with his old company and switched over to Quorum.

A Window of Opportunity

When a heavy hitter like Jeff Olson switches MLM companies, millions of phone lines across America light up with the news. It wasn't long before Freddie Rick heard through the grapevine that his idol had gone over to Quorum. Here was his chance! Freddie vowed immediately that he would join Jeff's downline in the new company.

"I called him several times," says Freddie, "but couldn't get through. Finally his wife called me and I ended up meeting with Jeff in Los Angeles. I was sponsored directly to him."

The Five-Year Plan

Through his vision and persistence, Freddie had suddenly become a frontline distributor for one of the top leaders in one of the fastest-growing network marketing companies in history. Not bad for an ex-sniper with $150,000 in debt and a job breaking heads in a sleazy nightclub. But there was a lot more to Freddie than what showed on the surface. And Jeff Olson saw that more clearly than most.

"Jeff believed in me before I believed in myself," says Freddie. "And because he believed in me, I wanted to do good."

Jeff taught Freddie the Slight Edge philosophy. He taught him that "time either promotes you or exposes you," that the Slight Edge was always working, either for you or against you. Freddie had been knocked around enough times to see the wisdom of that. He drank in Jeff's teachings as if they were nectar from Olympus.

"He taught me that I didn't have to achieve perfection tomorrow," says Freddie. "If I could just improve three-tenths of a percent every single day, I'd be 1600 percent better in five years."

Ten Pages a Day

Freddie was no scholar. The last book he could remember reading was *Charlie and the Chocolate Factory* sometime back in his childhood. But, inspired by the Slight Edge, Freddie committed to reading ten pages per day of whatever self-help literature Jeff recommended.

"I couldn't read that well," Freddie recalls. "But I knew if I kept up my ten pages a day, time would promote me. I just about memorized *Think and Grow Rich* by Napoleon Hill. I went to every seminar, listened to every tape, and read everything I could to improve myself. I got real familiar with names like Brian Tracy, Dr. Denis Waitley, Jim Rohn, and Anthony Robbins."

Under Jeff's tutelage, Freddie reached the top position in Quorum in only 13 months. By the time he finally left that company in 1994, Freddie's 1099 form gave his income for the year as $261,013.83. Freddie hadn't yet become a millionaire. But he was getting closer by the day. And 1999 was still five years away.

The Missing Link

Of course, Freddie Rick wasn't the only student in Jeff's school of self-help. At least ten of Jeff's frontline distributors had applied themselves to the Slight Edge regimen. Their need for training and motivation was nearly constant. With his travel schedule growing more intense by the day, Jeff was afraid he would not be able to give them adequate attention.

Technology came to the rescue. Just at that time, private satellite broadcasts were becoming cost-effective for network marketers. More and more upline leaders were beaming out training sessions and business briefings by satellite TV. Jeff told his top distributors to go out and buy satellite dishes. He started taping his trainings in a Dallas studio and broadcasting them every Monday night to his frontline.

To Jeff's amazement, his little satellite network grew to tens of thousands overnight. Distributors were forking over $500 cash for satellite dishes without a second thought, just so they could hear what Jeff had to say once a week.

"That made me stop and think," says Jeff. "If they would do that, just to hear *me*, what would they do to hear the really big guys, like Brian Tracy?"

Jeff had asked the billion-dollar question. Personal development happens to be one of the biggest and fastest-growing industries today, with an estimated $31 billion market in books, tapes, and seminars. A whole spectrum of television channels specialize in sports, news, cartoons, Congressional minutes, and just about everything else you can imagine. But, until Jeff Olson put his big idea to work, there was no such thing as a TV channel where people could view self-help programming that would coach them on how to improve their lives, health, and finances. Jeff realized that satellite technology was the key. It was the missing link in the business plan that he and Eric Worre had fashioned four years before as they sat by the swimming pool of the Shadow Mountain resort in Scottsdale.

The Peoples Network

Shortly thereafter, Jeff Olson and Eric Worre launched their new company, The Peoples Network—called TPN for short—a private satellite TV network featuring 100 percent motivational programming. Personal development giants such as Brian Tracy, Jim Rohn, and Les Brown got involved on the ground floor, contributing programming and selling their books and tapes through the TPN catalog. The satellite dishes and subscriptions were to be distributed through word-of-mouth alone by an army of eager network marketers.

Selling the Dream

"When TPN first came out," says distributor Michael S. Clouse, "we had nothing to hang our hats on. We had no programming, no one earning any income, no testimonials. We were selling a dream that didn't even exist yet. So we had to create a story that began with the word, 'Imagine . . .'"

Imagine having the most brilliant minds in the world coaching you on a day-to-day basis, TPN distributors would tell their prospects. *Imagine that you wouldn't have to fly, drive, or go anywhere to get this information. Imagine that these coaches would come to your home, fitting their coaching time into your busy schedule.*

We've all been to self-help seminars. But, after the seminar, it's hard to stay on track. You have nobody correcting and adjusting you from day to day, to keep you moving toward your goals. TPN will fill that gap.

Intangible as it seemed, the TPN story fired imaginations. People flocked to become distributors and subscribers. By the time the first broadcast went on the air on February 5, 1995, thousands were watching in living rooms across the country. It seemed that American television was about to get its next major network.

Losing the Vision

But then a strange thing happened. TPN nearly stumbled on its own success. As the company picked up steam in the early months, many distributors started raking in big money. The head office seized on these success stories eagerly. No longer would distributors have to entice their prospects with the word *Imagine*. Now they could show dollars and cents.

"The company issued a prospecting video emphasizing the incredible income opportunity," says Clouse, "and featuring all the success stories. Every distributor bought mass numbers of these videos and circulated them like crazy. The whole culture of the company started to shift. When you went to a business briefing now, it felt like 'rah rah, money money money.' But it backfired. People didn't like it." Recruitment in Clouse's organization slowed down tremendously.

Back to the Cause

It turned out that people were not joining TPN for the money. They were joining it for the Cause. The letters pouring in from distributors did not boast about how many subscriptions they were selling. They told about the little girl who came home with a report card showing a grade point average two full points higher than it had been the previous September because she watched TPN. They told of people who stopped smoking and drinking after subscribing to TPN, of estranged husbands and wives who came back together.

"We made a mistake," Jeff Olson announced to his field force during his televised Monday-night business briefing. "Now we're going to fix it. We've got a brand-new presentation and videotape coming out, and we're going to focus on what we believe people really want to hear and what we are being told by the field."

When the new video appeared, it contained a lot less talk about money. Instead, it featured testimonials to TPN's real achievement—better marriages, better families, better lives.

"You could hardly watch it without getting choked up," says Clouse. "When you go to a TPN business briefing today, it tugs at your heart. We've gone back to the Cause. Our Cause is to find a way to help you become happier, healthier, and more successful in every way."

Time Rewards Purpose

In many respects, TPN is an experiment. Neither the network marketing industry nor the world of conventional media has ever seen anything quite like it. As with most experiments, TPN's early days were fraught with trial and error. Just about everything went wrong in the first year that possibly could. Satellite dishes didn't ship on time. Computer systems failed. Checks went out late. But, through it all, TPN's downline maintained a retention rate that was one of the highest in the MLM industry, according to Jeff Olson.

This rock-like loyalty is a testament to one of Jeff's bedrock success principles: *Time looks for your purpose.* If you serve a real need, Jeff believes, time will forgive many mistakes along the way. Ultimately, it will reward you with success.

A Real Need

For Jeff, few needs in network marketing were more urgent than creating a company that could thrive without "frontloading"—pressuring distributors to spend a fortune stockpiling inventory. Only then would the industry really start working for the Freddie Ricks of this world. Only then would it fulfill its original promise to give ordinary people a chance to attain financial freedom.

"At TPN, your qualifier is equal to what you consume each month," says Jeff. "Anything that you purchase above that is because you are consuming more or you know somebody who wants some of the product. You can't buy a position in our company. We don't allow it."

Collaborative Economic Model

It is Jeff's ambition to build TPN along the lines of a "collaborative economic model"—a subculture whose members support one another through mutual trade. Over time, TPN has added nutritional and other personal care products to its catalog. Eventually, Jeff hopes his distributors will buy a wide range of necessary products through TPN, supporting the whole community, much as Mormons and Hasidic Jews support their communities and way of life by buying from each other whenever possible.

The Gyroscope

In keeping with that vision, Jeff recently decided that satellite dishes will now be given to new distributors free of charge, rather than sold for $500 a pop. In addition, TPN subscriptions (once $50 per month) will now be provided free to any distributor who commits to buying at least $50 per month worth of merchandise from TPN's World Mall, a catalog offering more than 400 different products, from skincare and nutritionals to books, tapes, and computer software. The satellite system itself is no longer a product, but has evolved into an indispensable link in the TPN infrastructure—the glue that binds this remarkable company together.

"No other direct sales company has a satellite link between its president and every single distributor in the field," says Jeff. "That has never happened before. We have our own production facilities, our own uplink, and our own transponder. We have a private studio right next to my office so that 24 hours a day, seven days a week, I can walk right in there, turn on the camera, and talk to the field."

Jeff likens the satellite system to a gyroscope.

"A rocket on its way to the moon is off track 97 percent of the time," he explains. "It's on track only 3 percent of the time. But it's always adjusting. In network marketing, the gyroscope used to be real loose. You could have a corporate event once every 90 days. You could see the owner of the company once or twice a year. Now my distributors can see me every Monday night when I do a special show, and they can see trainings every night.

"That allows us to keep a real tight gyroscope. Our people don't wander. They don't stray off track very often."

The "Slight Edge" Path

According to Jeff Olson, those who embark on the Slight Edge path can count on attaining their goals within five years. It may perhaps be more than coincidence that Freddie Rick and Jeff Olson both set out on their respective journeys in 1990—the year that Jeff and Eric Worre first dreamed of The Peoples Network and Freddie Rick pawned his nine-millimeter pistol. Five years to the day after Jeff and Freddie embarked on their separate Slight Edge paths, both achieved their dreams—in large measure, thanks to one another.

Not surprisingly, Freddie Rick was one of the first distributors to climb onboard the new company. It didn't take him until 1999 to become a millionaire. Empowered by TPN's unique electronic community, Freddie not only made his first million by 1995, but also became the top income earner in the company.

"Freddie has come a long, long way since I first met him," comments Jeff, "and, in a lot of respects, he still has a long way to go. But if he stays on the Slight Edge path, I have no doubt that Freddie will eventually smooth out his rough edges and acquire the kind of professionalism that will make him one of the top people in this industry."

Not every network marketer can count on finding a coach like Jeff Olson. Few have the faith and persistence to pursue their dream sponsor as tirelessly as did Freddie Rick. But, in an era when media and telecommunications are advancing more rapidly than ever, the time is growing near when no one will ever again need to fail for want of a teacher. Whether in TPN or in a score of other companies now experimenting with satellite training programs, the model of electronic sponsorship Jeff Olson and Eric Worre have established will likely be followed for many years to come.

Chapter 12

NOAH'S ARK

Vern Steyer winced at the voice he heard on the other end of his intercom phone. It was the principal of the school, angry and shouting, as usual.

"Steyer!" cried the principal. "Is it true that one of the kids you're counseling got shot with a pellet out at ROTC this morning?"

Vern sighed. "I really couldn't tell you, Jerry. I haven't heard about that."

"Well I want you to investigate that and have a report on my desk tomorrow morning."

The intercom phone clicked off. Vern sat for a long time, glaring at the wall, his face growing redder and hotter by the minute. *Why did he call me?* thought Vern. *Why is he always dragging me into things? I'm not the ROTC teacher. It takes the same amount of energy to call me as it does to call the ROTC teacher.*

Vern was not a happy man. It didn't take much these days to get him going. Even now, he could feel his heart rattling in his chest, like an old jalopy engine with a bad spark plug or two. *I can't take this much longer,* Vern thought to himself. *I really can't take it.*

The Monday Morning Massacre

Vern was right. His job as a high school counselor was literally killing him. Vern had already suffered one heart attack.

Just about once every three or four months now, he found himself back in the emergency room with yet another bout of chest pain or arrhythmia. The problem wasn't Vern's work. Vern loved kids and loved teaching. But he didn't have much use for bosses. Especially this particular boss.

Vern was not alone in his dilemma. Statistics show that more fatal and first-time heart attacks occur at 9 A.M. Monday morning than at any other time in the week. For many people, the stress of the 40-hour work week is more than their physiology can take.

Network marketing offers plenty of stress of its own. But for thousands—maybe millions—of people like Vern Steyer, it also offers a unique escape from need, worry, and the million little indignities that go with jumping at a boss's command. For many people, these benefits alone can make life worth living. For some, like Vern, they are life itself.

A Dramatic Shift

Not long ago, Vern ran into Martha, the nurse at his old school, in a local shopping mall. More than most, Martha knew Vern's suffering. He would usually head straight to her office when his heart started fluttering. After chatting for awhile, Martha blurted out the question that was uppermost on her mind.

"Okay, Vern, now that you're retired, how many visits have you had to the emergency room?"

Vern smiled. "You know, Martha, come to think of it, I haven't been there once."

The Golden Years

After retiring a few years back, Vern became a distributor for Excel Telecommunications (see Chapter 9). Now he works only a few hours a week, whenever he chooses. He spends all the time he wants with his grandson. And, after three years in the business, he enjoys a retirement income beyond anything he ever expected.

"After 32 years in public education," says Vern, "I had earned a pension that would allow me to exist but not to have any of the finer things in life. Now I have reached the level that my income from Excel no longer supplements my retirement. My retirement supplements my Excel income.

"What I like about this business is that it gives me the ability to do what I want to do, when I want to do it, and not have somebody glaring over my shoulder and making idiotic demands. I'm just thoroughly enjoying my life. My two daughters are very amused at me. They're always saying that Dad has really found his niche. He has really found his thing."

FREEDOM—WHEN YOU NEED IT MOST

Richard Kall learned the hard way that money can't solve every problem. But he also learned that the problems you have can be a lot easier to handle, when you have a hefty residual income.

Richard's wife, Carol, had stood by his side through thick and thin. She had raised a family with him, scrounged and scrabbled with him through one network marketing failure after another, and finally shared his triumph when they struck pay dirt with a company called NuSkin (see Chapter 4). Earning an annual income in the millions, the Kalls settled back to enjoy what they hoped would be many years of well-earned rest together. But their lazy days in the sun ended all too quickly when Carol was suddenly diagnosed with cancer.

What followed was an unending nightmare that lasted for years. Richard flew his wife to clinics all over the world, pursuing every experimental, alternative treatment that offered any hope. Sometimes she would seem to get better for a while. But her relapses always followed with merciless consistency.

At one point, Richard and Carol spent several weeks at a clinic in the Bahamas. The treatment was very expensive, and Richard noticed that the other couples at the clinic were all well-to-do.

"Everybody dressed well at this place," Richard recalls. "Everybody had money."

As he and Carol sat one day in the waiting room, Richard couldn't help overhearing a phone call going on about 12 feet away. A very prosperous-looking silver-haired man in his mid-50s, obviously a high-level corporate executive, was deep in a tense conversation with his office. His wife—a cancer patient—looked on worriedly.

At last, the man hung up the phone, put his hand on his forehead and turned to his wife in misery.

"Honey, I'm sorry," he said. "It's the stockholders. If I don't get back there right now, I'm out of a job."

Richard had noticed that with most of the couples at the clinic, it was the wife, not the husband, who had cancer. Now, as he looked around the room, he could see fear in the faces of many women in the room as they asked themselves, "How long will it be before my husband tells me the same thing?"

With all their money and power, Richard realized, the men in that room were little better than highly paid servants obligated to jump when their bosses cracked the whip. Richard reached over and squeezed Carol's hand. "We are so lucky," he said in her ear, and Carol nodded. Year after year, ever since the onset of her illness, she and Richard had been together 24 hours a day. It was impossible for Richard to spend the kind of time on his NuSkin business that he used to. Yet, month after month, the checks just kept coming in.

No amount of money in the world could compensate for his wife's loss of health. But the residual income Richard had earned from network marketing had come through for him in his time of greatest need.

NOAH'S ARK

"The time to repair the roof," said John F. Kennedy, "is when the sun is shining."

When God warned Noah to start building an ark, no one could have foreseen or imagined the torrential downpour that was on its way. Noah's massive shipbuilding project must have been a great source of wonder and hilarity to the neighbors.

But when the rains came down and the waters rose, those neighbors must have sung a different tune. As the great ark shifted loose from its moorings and started to drift, there must have been hundreds of fists pounding on the hull, a thousand voices raised in panicky pleas to be rescued. But it was too late. The ark was sealed and on its way. The chance to be saved had long since passed.

Modern-Day Noahs

In our turbulent economic times, we face a situation not unlike Noah's. Every sign points to rough waters ahead. As we make the traumatic shift to an Information Society, tens of millions are being cast into the street by corporations who no longer need their obsolete skills.

Many of the displaced are our loved ones. They are aged parents facing retirement with inadequate pensions. They are brothers and sisters struggling to feed their families. They're our children, fresh out of college, trying to make their way in a world that no longer offers secure employment.

Noah's heart must have burst with sorrow as he listened to the cries of the drowning, knowing they could not be saved. But those who build network marketing businesses today can do something that Noah couldn't. They can reach out a hand to their struggling friends and loved ones and pull them aboard to safety.

Ignore the Laughter

Every network marketer knows how it feels to be laughed at. They know how Noah must have felt when he and his family were building that ark amid the derision of the neighbors. But, like Noah, with every prospecting call you make and every recruit you train, you are building an escape vehicle for the coming flood. You are building an infrastructure of knowledge, experience, and skill uniquely adapted for life in the cutthroat economy of the 21st century.

Someday—perhaps someday soon—those you love most will come swimming out of the floodwaters to pound on the side of your ark and cry out for help. Unlike Noah, you'll be able to pull them aboard. Those who have never learned what it means to be their own boss, to survive in the marketplace, and to build a business from scratch will look to you for the necessary skills. And you will have them to give.

VENUS'S NIGHTMARE

One night, Venus Andrecht had a terrible nightmare. In her dream, her network marketing company had gone out of business and she had been forced to go back to her old job.

"What an awful dream!" Venus thought, when she awoke.

But it was only a dream. Back in reality, Venus was once again a top distributor for her company, earning $25,000 to $30,000 each month. Indeed, Venus was something of an MLM celebrity. She appeared frequently in industry trade journals as a columnist and interview subject. Her training seminars attracted a nationwide clientele from every company in the business, and her best-selling books, such as *MLM Magic and Prospecting: How to Find 'Em, Sign 'Em, and What to Do with 'Em in Multilevel,* were beloved by thousands. Yet, after her nightmare, Venus found it hard to shake the feeling that her bubble was about to burst.

A Mysterious Warning

It wasn't long after that that Venus had a strange encounter in the supermarket. As she was making her way down the aisles, an old woman walked up, stood right in front of Venus, and locked eyes with her.

"I've read about you in the newspaper," said the woman.

Venus wasn't surprised. In the little California town where she lives, the local newspaper frequently runs features on Venus, keeping residents advised of her every move. Still, she had never seen this woman before and wasn't sure who she was.

"I want you to promise me something," said the old woman, holding up one bony finger. "Promise me you'll save every penny, because you never know what's going to happen. Promise me!"

Venus promised and the woman went away.

"I had no idea who this woman was, but I figured this must have happened for a reason, so I started saving my money."

A Rainy Day

The proverbial rainy day hit about a year later. At Christmastime in 1994, one of her fellow distributors called Venus in a panic.

"Have you heard the news?" she said. "Our company has gone bankrupt. None of our checks will be coming through. It's all over."

In the end, the company managed to survive its cashflow crisis. But, at the time, it seemed like the end of the world to people like Venus Andrecht who had staked their entire livelihood on it. Even harder hit were many people in Venus's downline, who had been earning far more modest incomes than she.

"It was very upsetting," she recalls. "One man lost everything and told me he'd considered suicide. Two friends of mine whom I'd recruited into the business told me they were going to lose their houses. There were people with six kids, people with college tuitions to pay. I was just horrified. I was shocked to find that so many people didn't have any savings. They lived from check to check, even people who'd been getting very big checks. They'd spent every cent and hadn't put anything away."

No Cure-All

Ultimately, Venus switched to another company and rebuilt her MLM business. She is now a Double Diamond with Cell Tech. But the experience chastened her.

To this day, Venus has no idea who that old woman was in the supermarket, but she owes her a great debt of gratitude. Had Venus not begun saving money a year in advance of the crisis, she too would have been in as bad a position as some of her downline.

The lesson is: Network marketing is no cure-all. But, with a modicum of good sense and planning, it just might prove to be the critical factor enabling you and yours to ride out the economic storms ahead. More than any other business in existence, network marketing enables the common man to reach out his hand and touch the stars. By the amazing power of the Butterfly Effect, you can learn to send waves of power and wealth rippling through your downline with the faintest of gestures. But, with that same light touch, ruin and despair can sweep your downline with equal force. Remember that the Wave Three Way is a path of leadership. Walk it gingerly, with compassion and love. Walk it gravely and responsibly. For many are the lives who depend on you to walk it well.

INDEX

The Einstein Factor

Win Wenger, Ph.D., and Richard Poe

U.S. $15.95
Can. $21.95

"Brainpower and intuition are key to success in network marketing. Every leader in every network marketing company should invest in The Einstein Factor *and practice its remarkable techniques. . . . It's that good!"*

—Michael S. Clouse, editor-in-chief, *Upline*

"The Einstein Factor *is a winner. It should go to every man, woman, and child in the land . . . a fine, yeasty book."*

—Lynn Schroeder, co-author,
Superlearning and *Superlearning 2000*

"To excel in network marketing, you have to become several kinds of 'smart.' The techniques in The Einstein Factor *will give you access to your inner genius and permanently increase the caliber of your mind. Indispensable for leaders in any business."*

—Duncun Maxwell Anderson, senior editor, *Success* magazine

"Wow! Success *readers love this book.* The Einstein Factor *has skyrocketed to become our number-one bestseller for 1996—and no wonder, as its scientifically based techniques are both remarkably powerful and amazingly simple to apply."*

—*Success* magazine